The Mandelstam and "Der Nister" Files

The Mandelstam and "Der Nister" Files

An Introduction to Stalin-era Prison and Labor Camp Records

Peter B. Maggs

M.E. Sharpe
Armonk, New York
London, England

Library of Congress Cataloging-in-Publication Data

Maggs, Peter B.
The Mandelstam and "Der Nister" files : an introduction to
Stalin-era prison and labor camp records / by Peter B. Maggs.
p.   cm.
Includes bibliographical references and index.
ISBN 1-56324-175-7 (alk. paper)
1. Prison administration—Soviet Union—History—Sources.
2. Labor camps—Soviet Union—History—Sources.
3. Soviet Union—Politics and government—1936–1953—Sources.
4. Mandel'shtam, Osip, 1891–1938. 5. Der Nister, 1884–1950.
6. Poets, Russian—20th century—Biography.
7. Poets, Yiddish—Ukraine—Biography. I. Title.
HV9712.M34   1995
365'.45'0947—dc20   95-41480
CIP

Printed in the United States of America

The paper used in this publication meets the minimum requirements of
American National Standard for Information Sciences—
Permanence of Paper for Printed Library Materials,
ANSI Z 39.48-1984.

CONTENTS

List of Documents   vii

List of Acronyms   ix

Introduction   3

Osip Emilevich Mandelstam   5
Pinchas Mendelevich Kahanovitch   6
Soviet Government Agencies Dealing with
    Political Prisoners   7

About the Documents

A Prisoner's Personal File: Cover and Cover Page   9
Order to Receive a Prisoner   10
Decision on the Selection of a Measure of Restraint   12
The Search Record   15
Arrestee Form   17
Intake Fingerprint Form   17
Preconviction Transfer to Another Prison   18
Search on Prison Transfer   19
Prisoner Photographs   20
Permission to Receive Items   20
Prisoner Interrogation Records   21
Extension of Detention   25

The Decision to Send to a Special Camp   26
The Decision of the Special Board   27
The Prisoner's Acknowledgment of Receipt of the
    Decision of the Special Board   30
Notice   31
Transfer to Being Held for the Special Board   31
Order to Transfer to a Labor Camp   32
Camp Records—Form No. 1   33
Certification on Property   35
Medical Treatment   36
Death Certificates   38
Postmortem Fingerprinting   38
Burial   40
Correspondence with Relatives   42

Concluding Thoughts   47

Notes   49

The Documents

Documents follow page 50

LIST OF DOCUMENTS

Mandelstam File Contents

M–0	Cover
M–1	File Header
M–2	Form No. 1 (Statistical-Record Card)
M–2BACK	Form No. 1 (Account of Working Days by Camps)
M–3	Excerpt from Record of the Special Board
M–4	Coupon of Arrest Warrant
M–5	Prisoner Transfer Record
M–6	Photo Card (on back of File Header)
M–7	Record of Identity of Fingerprints
M–8	Form No. 2 (Fingerprint Form)
M–9	Note on Time of Death
M–10	Form No. 2 (Post-Mortem Fingerprints)
M–11	Death Certificate
M–12	Letter from Nadezhda Mandelstam
M–13	Form No. 77 (Memorandum of July 20, 1939)
M–14	Death Confirmation
M–15	Form No. 77 (Memorandum of August 22, 1939)
M–16	Form No. 1 (Statistical-Record Card)—Camp Arrival

Kaganovich File Contents

K–0	Cover
K–1	Notice on Sending to Special Camp
K–1BACK	Notice on Sending to Special Camp
K–2	Coupon of Arrest Warrant

K–3   Order on the Selection of a Measure of Restraint (front)
K–3BACK   Order on the Selection of a Measure of Restraint (back)
K–4/5   Arrestee Form (items 1–11)
K–4/5   Arrestee Form (items 12–14)
K–4/5   Arrestee Form (items 15–20)
K–4/5   Arrestee Form (signature page)
K–6   Form No. 2 (Fingerprint Form)
K–7   Medical Certificate
K–8   Search Record
K–9   Prison Transfer Record
K–10   Medical Certificate
K–11   Search Record
K–12   Extension of Term of Detention to May 19, 1949
K–13   Extension of Term of Detention to June 19, 1949
K–14   Medical Conclusion
K–15   Medical Conclusion Forwarding
K–16   Extension of Term of Detention to August 19, 1949
K–17   Medical Report
K–18   Permission to Receive Clothing
K–19   Extension of Term of Detention to July 19, 1949
K–20   Reassignment to Special Board
K–21   Excerpt from the Record of the Special Board
K–22   Order on Sending to a Special Camp
K–23   Decision to Send to a Special Camp
K–24   Memorandum on Non-Confiscation of Property
K–25   Photographs
K–26   Attachment No. 3 to Order
K–27/28   Personal File Form No. 1 (Sections I–II)
K–27/28   Personal File Form No. 1 (Sections III–IV)
K–27/28   Personal File Form No. 1 (Sections V–VI)
K–27/28   Personal File Form No. 1 (Section VII)
K–29   Certificate of Death
K–30   Certificate of Burial
K–31   Report of Death
K–32   First Page of History of Illness
K–85   Request to Call Prisoner for Questioning

LIST OF ACRONYMS

GUGB (Glavnoe upravlenie gosudarstvennoi bezopasnosti)—Main Administration of State Security

GULAG (Glavnoe upravlenie lagerei)—Main Administration of [Labor] Camps

ITL (Ispravitel´no-trudovoi lager´)—corrective labor camp

KGB (Komitet gosudarstvennoi bezopasnosti)—Committee for State Security

KPZ (Kamera predvaritel´nogo zakliucheniia)—preliminary detention facility

KRD (kontrrevoliutsionnaia deiatel´nost´)—counterrevolutionary activity

MGB (Ministerstvo gosudarstvennoi bezopasnosti)—Ministry of State Security

MVD (Ministerstvo vnutrennikh del)—Ministry of Internal Affairs

NKGB (Narodnyi komissariat gosudarstvennoi bezopasnosti)—People's Commissariat of State Security

NKVD (Narodnyi komissariat vnutrennikh del)—People's Commissariat of Internal Affairs

OAGS (Otdel aktov grazhdanskogo sostoianiia)—Department of Registration of Civil Status

OLP (Otdel lagernykh poliklinik)—Department of Camp Clinics

OUR (Otdel ugolovnogo rozyska)—Department of Criminal Investigation

OVD (Otdel vnutrennykh del)—Department of Internal Affairs

OVD (Osobenno vazhnye dela)—Especially Important Cases

RO (Raspredelitel´nyi otdel)—Assignment Department

SVITL (Severo-vostochnyi ispravitel´no-trudovye lagery)—Northeast Corrective Labor Camps

UGB (Upravlenie gosudarstvennoi bezopasnosti)—Administration of State Security

UMGB (Upravlenie Ministerstva gosudarstvennoi bezopasnosti)—Administration of the Ministry of State Security

UNKVD (Upravlenie Narodnogo komissariata vnutrennikh del)—Administration of the People's Commissariat of Internal Affairs

URCh (Uchetno-raspredelitel´naia chast´)—Accounting and Assignment Section

URO (Uchetno-raspredelitel´nyi: otdel)—Accounting Assignment Department

USO (Upravlenie statisticheskogo otdela)—Administration of the Statistical Department

USVITL (Upravlenie Severo-vostochnykh ispravitel´no-trudovykh lagerei)—Administration of Northeast Corrective Labor Camps

ZAGS ([Biuro] Zapisei aktov grazhdanskogo sostoianiia)—Civil State Registry

The
Mandelstam
and
"Der Nister"
Files

INTRODUCTION

*"Who is likely to search through these grisly archives
just for the sake of Mandelstam . . . ?"*
—Nadezhda Mandelstam

This book tells three stories. The first is what prison and labor-camp files reveal of the history of the great poet Osip Mandelstam from the time a warrant was issued for his arrest in April 1938 until the time his relatives were notified of his death in 1940. The second is what the files reveal of the history of the major Yiddish writer Der Nister (pseudonym of Pinchas Kahanovitch) from the time of his arrest in February 1949 until his burial in July 1950. The third is a guided tour through Stalin-era prison and labor-camp records, designed to expose more fully the horrors of the system and to help researchers find their way through the records of other victims of Soviet socialist "justice."

This book is based on two files from the USSR Ministry of Internal Affairs archives. The consistency of the documents with one another and with external evidence suggests that they are genuine, in the sense that they were made at the time at which they are dated by those whose signatures appear on them. However, these documents certainly do not tell the truth, let alone the whole truth. They do not tell the truth, because they are based on what George Orwell called the "BIG LIE"—that Mandelstam and Der Nister were guilty of serious crimes. They do not tell the whole truth—they give no hint as to the real reason why the two writers were sent to labor camps. They supply neither confirmation nor refutation for various widely circulated rumors: that Mandelstam was shot; that Mandelstam lived on in the camps after the official date of his "death"; that Der Nister hid important unpublished manuscripts. These files contain administrative, not substantive materials. From them, we can learn much about how prisoners were processed but very little about the charges against the prisoners.

The documents are presented in pairs, consisting of a photograph of the original Russian document and an accompanying English translation, the latter roughly matching the original Russian in layout and typefaces. The order of presentation is generally chronological, proceeding from arrest, through the prisons, to the labor camp, and then to the grave. Almost every one of the documents in the files bears a reference number (probably added relatively recently) in the upper right corner. References in this book are by these numbers—documents M–1, M–2, and so forth, relate to Mandelstam; documents K–1, K–2, and so forth, relate to Kahanovitch (Der Nister).

Both names have many spellings. In the text, I have adopted the form "Osip Emilevich Mandelstam," which is common in English-language works about the poet. In the text, I use "Pinchas Kahanovitch," which is how the Library of Congress catalogs his works, or the pseudonym Der Nister, for which there is luckily only one spelling in English-language works. In translating the documents I have presented the spelling used in the original documents in a modified Library of Congress transliteration. I have reproduced spelling errors in the original documents, to reflect the irony of semiliterate jailors processing extraordinarily literate writers.

Osip Emilevich Mandelstam

Osip Mandelstam was born in Warsaw (which was then in the Russian Empire) in 1891. His education included formal study in St. Petersburg, France, and Germany and very extensive reading. He began writing poetry while a student and soon was recognized as one of Russia's greatest poets. In 1933 he read to friends a poem satirizing Stalin. This led to his arrest in 1934, to his conviction for "counter-revolutionary activity," and to exile to various provincial towns. His second and final arrest came on May 2, 1938. His death certificate is dated December 27, 1939. His widow, Nadezhda Mandelstam, wrote memoirs of their life together that occupy as lofty a place in modern Russian prose, as does his own work in Russian poetry.[1]

Pinchas Kahanovitch

Pinchas Kahanovitch was born 1884 in Berdichev, Ukraine. Early in his writing career, he took on the Yiddish pseudonym Der Nister meaning "The Hidden One." He is generally regarded as one of the leading Yiddish writers of the twentieth century. During the period 1907–18, he published poems, songs, and prayers and translated Hans Christian Andersen. His writing in the early 1920s, when he lived in Berlin, was in the tradition of Jewish mysticism. He returned to the Soviet Union in 1929 and began writing in a more realistic style. The first volume of his masterwork *Di Mishpoke Mashber* (The Family Mashber) was published in Yiddish in the Soviet Union in 1939. It was an account of Berdichev in his parents' time. He was arrested in February 1949 and died in a labor camp on June 4, 1950.[2]

Soviet Government Agencies
Dealing with Political Prisoners

During the 1930s and 1940s there were a number of reorganizations and renamings of the agencies handling state security.[3] At the time of Mandelstam's arrest, both ordinary and political arrestees were subject to the jurisdiction of the People's Commissariat of Internal Affairs, called NKVD—the acronym for *Narodnyi komissariat vnutrennikh del*. A division of the NKVD, the Main Administration for State Security, GUGB—*Glavnoe upravlenie gosudarstvennoi bezopasnosti*—handled political prisoners. During World War II the state security organization achieved separate status as the People's Commissariat of State Security, NKGB—*Narodnyi komissariat gosudarstvennoi bezopasnosti*. Then in 1946, in an attempt to sound less revolutionary and so gain international respectability, Stalin had the "people's commissariats" renamed "ministries," with the result that the "NK" in each Russian acronym became an "M." So the People's Commissariat of Internal Affairs (NKVD) became the Ministry of Internal Affairs (MVD) and the People's Commissariat of State Security (NKGB) became the Ministry of State Security (MGB)—see Document K–7, where an old NKGB form has been recycled by handwriting an "M" over the "NK." The eventual successor of the MGB was the Committee on State Security—the infamous KGB. Throughout the 1930s and 1940s, however, the labor camps remained under the jurisdiction of the NKVD and its successor, the MVD. The agency in charge of them was the Main Administration of Labor Camps, known as "GULAG"—short for *glavnoe upravlenie lagerei*.

The separation of the MGB and MVD meant a separation of records. A prisoner's arrest, prison, and labor-camp records ended up in the labor-camp administrative offices—in Mandelstam's case in Magadan, the administrative center for labor camps in the Russian Far East and subordinate to the MVD. His interrogation records remained with the state security organization and ended up in the hands of the KGB. The files discussed in this book are those from the MVD archives.

ABOUT THE DOCUMENTS

■ A Prisoner's Personal File: Cover and Cover Page

Personal files were opened for Mandelstam and Der Nister upon their arrest. The file header (Document M–1) was made at Butyrka Prison, where, it states, Mandelstam arrived on August 4, 1938. Various numbers are written on this cover page in various hands. The number V/3–2844 on this page is the permanent file number used on the documents in the Mandelstam file. Both files were stored in rather similar heavy brown outer covers. The outer cover that was on the Mandelstam file, Document M–0, dates from the 1960s, as is evident from two printed dates of "196_." The reason for a 1960s cover is a mystery. Perhaps the Magadan Archive reorganized its files. Perhaps someone in the Soviet government took an interest in the file and asked for it to be retrieved, at which time its custodians decided it needed a new, sturdy cover. The cover of Kahanovitch's file (Document K–0) seems to date from around the time of his arrest in 1949. Unlike the Mandelstam cover, it bears the classification "SE-CRET." It seems likely that stricter secrecy regulations were in effect in the 1940s than in the 1960s. The two dates on the file are February 20, 1949, the day after the date of his arrest warrant, and February 19, 1959, the date of the scheduled end of his term of imprisonment. The file number, 021594, appears at the top left of the cover. Lower and to the right is the word "convicted"— presumably added at some point after conviction. Obviously the admonition at the top left of the cover against adding extraneous writings was ignored.

The most notable writing on the file cover is "Jewish nationality" at the top right. Der Nister's arrest was clearly a part of the campaign against Yiddish culture that was launched in a campaign called *Zhdanovshchina* in 1947. By the time of Der Nister's arrest, the Ministry of State Security, acting on orders from Stalin and Andrei Zhdanov, already had arrested numerous leaders of Yiddish cultural life and had effectively closed down Yiddish publications. It is amazing that Der Nister survived arrest until 1949.[4]

■ Order to Receive a Prisoner

> *"[On May 2] we were wakened by somebody knocking quietly on the door. . . . "Do you know when it was signed?" M. asked me looking at the warrant. It appeared that it had been signed about a week previously. "It's not our fault," one of the men in uniform explained, "we have too much to do."*
> —Nadezhda Mandelstam, *Hope Against Hope: A Memoir*, trans. Max Hayward (New York: Atheneum, 1972), p. 361.

Under Soviet practice in the 1930s and 1940s, each arrest warrant came with an attached coupon. The warrant authorized the arresting agency to make the arrest. The coupon ordered the receiving agency to detain the arrestee. The arrest warrant was shown to Nadezhda Mandelstam. Presumably this warrant was then filed in the arrest files of the arresting agency. That is why the warrant is not in Mandelstam's file. What is in the file is the coupon (Document M–4), which orders the "Head of Reception of Arrestees" to receive the arrestee Mandelstam. It appears to have been normal practice to include the coupon in the file of the arrested person. The coupon is stamped "*Sfotografirovan*" (photographed). When arrested persons were brought in, they were routinely photographed. The photographs of both Mandelstam and Der Nister in these files will be discussed below.

The coupon tells us something of the organization of the state security apparatus in 1938. At this time, the People's Commissariat of Internal Affairs was responsible both for ordinary police work and for state security. State security was the responsibility of the Main Administration for State Security, which was directly subordinate to the People's Commissariat of Internal Affairs. Subordinate in turn to the Main Administration for State Security were departments, with the Second Department being responsible for this particular arrest. The form used appeared to be one meant for important arrests—it bears spaces for the signatures of the Deputy People's Commissar of Internal Affairs of the USSR and the Head of the Second Department of the Main Administration of State Security.

Russian legal terminology relating to arrests is complex and confusing.[5] The 1923 Criminal Procedure Code used the term *"zaderzhanie"* for what would be called "arrest" in Anglo-American legal terminology—taking a person into custody under authority of the law. The 1936 Constitution, on the other hand, uses the term *"arest."* The Main Administration of State Security used the Russian word *"arest"* rather than the Criminal Procedure Code term *"zaderzhanie."* The Russian original of Document M–4 is addressed *"Nachal'niku priema arestovannykh"*—"To the Head of Reception of Arrestees." It orders this official to receive the "arrestee" Mandelstam.

When the state security agents came for Der Nister in February 1949, he is reported to have said, "Thank God, you came at last. I have waited for you for so long."[6] According to his wife: "He received the N.K.V.D. with a broadly mocking smile which greatly irritated them. The officer who conducted the search began to laugh stupidly. . . . To this Der Nister said in Yiddish: 'Why are you angry? I am happy that you've come.' "[7]

Document K–2 is the coupon from the arrest warrant for Der Nister. It is on an updated form, differing in a number of respects from that used for Mandelstam's arrest. By the time of

Kahanovitch's arrest in 1949, there had been a number of organizational changes. As already noted, the Soviet Union had renamed each "people's commissariat" as a less revolutionary-sounding "ministry." A major organizational change had promoted the state security apparatus from a subordinate "main administration" under the Ministry of Internal Affairs to make it the "USSR Ministry of State Security." Thus it was this ministry that issued the arrest warrant for Kahanovitch.

The Der Nister arrest coupon, like the Mandelstam arrest coupon, bears the number of the respective arrest warrant to which it was attached. The Mandelstam coupon is dated April 30, 1938, which was a Saturday. It says it was attached to Arrest Warrant No. 2817. The Der Nister coupon is dated February 19, 1949, which was a Saturday. It says it was attached to Arrest Warrant No. 536. In both cases the numbers appear to have been stamped with a number-stamping machine of the type that automatically increments the number each time it is used. More research into the numbering system could be helpful in determining the total numbers of political arrests and in determining the completeness of files, since a missing number in the sequence would suggest a missing file.

■ Order on the Selection of a Measure of Restraint

The "ORDER (on the selection of a measure of restraint)," Document K–3, provides the formal legal justification for the continued holding of Der Nister. There is no similar document for Mandelstam. Since Der Nister's file is more complete than Mandelstam's, either some documents have been lost from Mandelstam's file, or, possibly, the smaller number of political arrests in 1949 allowed more time for complying with legal niceties. Pretrial detention of persons arrested by the state security authorities was subject to unpublished, secret rules. In theory, at least, these rules would have to comply with the Soviet Constitution. In practice, as applied in Der Nister's case, they appear to have been rather close to the general rules of the Criminal Procedure Code. Under the general provisions of the Criminal Procedure Code in effect at the time, "agencies of inquiry" had the power to detain a "suspect" on their own accord. Of course, in the case of both Mandelstam and Der Nister, the actual decision for their arrest was undoubtedly made not by the agencies of inquiry but by Stalin or someone carrying out his orders. The "agency of inquiry" in Mandelstam's case was the Main Administration of State Security of the People's Commissariat of Internal Affairs. As the result of reorganizations, this agency became the Second Main Administration of the Ministry of State Security of the USSR by the time of Der Nister's arrest.

Article 104 of the Russian Criminal Procedure Code provided:

> In all cases of detention of a suspect (Art. 100 of the Criminal Procedure Code), the agencies of inquiry shall, within twenty-four hours, send notification, with an indication of the bases of detention, to the investigator in whose district the agency of inquiry is located or to the nearest People's Judge.
>
> Within forty-eight hours, counting from the moment of receipt of notification from the agency of inquiry of notification about a detention that has occurred, the investigator or the People's Judge must confirm the detention or revoke it. Agencies of inquiry shall change the measure of restraint upon receipt of a corresponding notification from the agencies to which notification was sent.*
>
> *Note.* The procedure for approval of detentions made by agencies of the Joint State Political Administration† is determined by special rules established for it.

---

*In accordance with Art. 131 of the Constitution of the RSFSR, the approval of a procurator must be obtained for continued confinement under guard.

†The Ministry of State Security of the USSR.

Under the Criminal Procedure Code, an "agency of inquiry" had forty-eight hours after being notified of a detention to confirm or revoke the detention. An official note in the official edition of the Code indicates that special rules apply to detention by agencies of inquiry subordinate to state security organizations. These special rules (which were secret) probably also required a decision within forty-eight hours. The secret rules must have paralleled Article 146 in requiring a motivated decision on "adoption of a measure of restraint." Article 146 reads:

> Upon adoption of a measure of restraint, the investigator compiles a motivated decision, with an indication of the crime of which the given person is accused and of the bases for the adoption of one or another measure of restraint. The accused shall be informed immediately and the procurator shall be notified immediately of the taking of a measure of restraint.

Documents K–3 and K–3 BACK constitute this "motivated decision." Of course the investigator would not give the real motivation, which was an order from high political authorities, but rather a standard formal motivation, complying with the letter of the law. Thus the "motivation" given in each case is "might avoid investigation and trial."

Article 143 of the Criminal Procedure Code listed five possible "measures of restraint." These were

(1) a signed commitment not to depart,
(2) a personal and property guarantee,
(3) a pledge of property,
(4) house arrest, or
(5) detention under guard.

Probably these various measures of restraint were also available under the secret rules governing political cases. Any investigator would have realized that the arrest of such prominent figures as Mandelstam or Der Nister must have been ordered at a very high level, most likely personally by Stalin or Zhdanov. Whether or not privy to this order, the investigator certainly would have been afraid to release either Mandelstam or Kahanovitch. Thus the investigator could only choose "detention under guard" as the measure of restraint.

The following text appears following Article 146 in the editions of the Criminal Procedure Code published by the People's Commissariat of Justice and its successor, the Ministry of Justice:

> Note 1 to Art. 146, "The approval of a procurator is required for the adoption of detention under guard (see Art. 131 of the Constitution of the USSR)."

The top right of the form contains a space for the signature of the Deputy Procurator General of the USSR, Lieutenant General of Justice Vavilov, but there is no signature by him.

Article 160 of the Criminal Procedure Code states how detention under guard is implemented in ordinary civil cases:

> If the investigator selects, as a measure of restraint, detention under guard, the investigator shall inform the procurator and shall send a copy of the order to the place of detention and the place of work of the accused. . . .

These records show only a notification of the place of detention. Mandelstam did not have a regular place of work. While Kahanovitch still lived in the dormitory of the Yiddish Theater at the time of his arrest, it appears from the records that he was no longer employed on the staff there. Given the huge number of Soviet citizens who vanished during the purges, there is no reason to suppose that there was a practice of routine notification of the place of work. The files also show no evidence of notification of a procurator or of receipt of approval of a procurator. Failure to obtain such approval would have been a direct violation of Article 131 of the Stalin Constitution of 1936.

■ The Search Record

There is only one search record (Document K–8) in the files, that of the personal search of Kahanovitch upon his arrival at the

Internal Prison of the Ministry of State Security. (The ministry's main "Internal Prison" was Lubianka, but there was at least one other in Moscow.) Typically, when making an arrest, the Soviet authorities would search the residence of the arrestee for incriminating evidence. Then, as a matter of jail administration, the jailors would search each arriving prisoner for contraband. Any records of searches of the premises upon the arrests of Mandelstam and Kahanovitch would have gone not to their personal files (which are the subject of this book) but to their investigation files.

Unfortunately, the search records that went into the investigation files are not available. Were they available, they might provide some help in solving the mystery of the fate of the manuscript of Part III of Der Nister's novel *The Family Mashber*. According to his wife's memoirs, after sending Part II abroad to be published, he kept working on Part III. She wrote that her husband, in answer to a question by the arresting officers about where he had hidden his manuscripts, replied, "Forgive me, gentlemen, that matter is none of your concern. It was not for you that I wrote them, and my manuscripts remain in a safe place."[8] Since we do not have the investigation file, we do not know if the investigators found Part III of the novel.

It is a general practice in jail administration everywhere to search all arriving prisoners for weapons and other contraband. The Soviet security system was no exception. As provided in the arrest-warrant coupon dated February 19, 1949, Der Nister was taken to the Internal Prison of the Ministry of State Security, where he was searched on the same day. The search record reflects two procedural protections for the arrestee: a requirement that a witness be present during the search and countersign the search record, and a requirement that the arrestee sign the search record. The search procedure complied with these requirements. The search record reports that nothing was found. Kahanovitch's signature on the search record, as on all the other documents, is weak and shaky, suggesting that he was in bad health from the moment of his detention onward.

■ Arrestee Form

Soon after Der Nister arrived at the Internal Prison of the Ministry of State Security, the prison authorities filled out an Arrestee Form (Documents K–4/5) and a fingerprint form (Document K–6). Mandelstam's file contains a fingerprint form (Document M–8) and a photograph form (Document M–6) but no arrestee form. The Arrestee Form appears to have had two purposes: (1) to provide identifying information to allow those dealing with the prisoner to verify they have the right person; (2) to gather data that might be useful in investigation and sentencing. Identifying information included a "Portrait in Words" made by selecting one of half a dozen characteristics for "Height," "Figure," "Neck," "Hair color," and so on. The form also asks a number of questions of a general social and political nature, such as "Nationality," "Citizenship," "Party membership," "Education," and "Criminal record." Documents in Mandelstam's file indicate that similar questions were asked in the 1930s. This form also contains two new questions, obviously added during or after World War II, "Participation in the fatherland war (where, when, and as what)" (Question 12) and "Was he on territory occupied by the enemy (indicate: where, when and what he did)" (Question 13).

■ Intake Fingerprint Form

There is an intake fingerprint form for Mandelstam (Document M–8) and for Der Nister (Document K–6). The standard fingerprint form has two sets of fingerprints: a basic set, done finger by finger; and a "Check Print" of each hand (without thumbprints). Fingerprints were used for two very different purposes in the Soviet criminal law system. Investigators used fingerprint matching to solve crimes by comparing fingerprints left at the scene of the crime with those of suspects. The penal system used fingerprint matching to ensure that there was no substitution of persons confined in the system. Fingerprints were first taken at the arrival of a prisoner. They were then checked as the prisoner moved through the system as a means of verification that the prisoner was the person that his documents said he was. Mandelstam's intake fingerprint form (Document M–8) shows the unscarred hands of a poet. The quality of the fingerprints is excellent, reflecting the access of the state security jailers in Moscow to the best equipment. Russian practice was to code fingerprints with classification numbers to enable searching for matching sets of fingerprints. Der Nister's intake fingerprint form (Document K–6) shows the worn hands of an older man, including a severe scar on the middle finger of the right hand. (This scar is mentioned in answer to Question 16 on his Arrest Form Document K–5.)

Unlike Mandelstam's fingerprints, Der Nister's are not coded. Perhaps the state security authorities abandoned the practice of coding fingerprints of political prisoners. In the precomputer age, criminal investigation authorities kept files of fingerprints arranged by code numbers. When investigators found fingerprints at the scene of a crime, they could then code the fingerprints found and look at similar fingerprints cataloged under the same code number to try to find a match. Such a practice made sense for common criminals, such as burglars, who after serving a short sentence were likely to return to their criminal ways. However, for several reasons, this whole process made little sense for political prisoners. Few political prisoners ever emerged alive from the camps, and even if they got out and returned to a life of political crime, for instance, reciting anti-Stalin poetry, such activities were very unlikely to leave fingerprints.

■ Preconviction Transfer to Another Prison

Every transfer of a prisoner from one place of detention had to be documented. On August 5, 1938, Mandelstam was transferred to Butyrka Prison. The transfer record (Document M–5) shows that the transfer was ordered by the Tenth Department of the Main Administration of State Security of the People's Commissariat of Internal Affairs. Thus, if a prisoner's record is intact, it should be possible to reconstruct from the transfer records where the prisoner was held and under whose authority at each point of his detention. In case of an escape, the institution and authorities having custody at the time of the escape faced retribution.[9] It was very important to have records that showed, at all times, who was responsible. It was the practice to hold suspected co-conspirators in isolation from one another. Since the lines following the words "Isolated from arrestee(s) . . . " are blank, one may conclude that there was no one thought to be a "co-conspirator" with Mandelstam in detention at Butyrka at the time of the transfer.

A similar form (Document K–9) dated February 22, 1949, provides for the transfer of Der Nister from the Internal Prison of the Ministry of State Security to Lefortovo Prison, which was also under the jurisdiction of the Ministry of State Security. This form even instructs the receiving prison as to the cell where he is to be placed. No doubt the authorities of the two prisons had communicated beforehand to set up the transfer. This form, like that for Mandelstam, bears the inscription "TOP SECRET." Probably extreme secrecy was maintained about transfers because of the possibility that criminal associates of a prisoner could aid in an escape during a transfer, since it would be much easier to hijack a transfer van than to break into a heavily fortified and guarded prison.

■ Search on Prison Transfer

On February 22, 1949, the MGB transferred Der Nister from its Internal Prison to Lefortovo Prison. He thus joined the list of many great Stalin-era cultural figures who were sent to Lefortovo for interrogation. In addition to the transfer form, discussed above, there is also a record of the search of the prisoner on his arrival at Lefortovo (Document K–11). The search record states that nothing was found. This is not surprising. Since Kahanovitch must have been searched upon arrival at the Internal Prison of the MGB and was confined incommunicado there until the transfer to Lefortovo, he would have had no chance to acquire any contraband.

■ Prisoner Photographs

> *"M. froze in his leather coat, which by now*
> *[months after his arrest] was in tatters."*
> —Nadezhda Mandelstam, *Hope Against Hope: A Memoir*,
> trans. Max Hayward (New York: Atheneum, 1972), p. 380.

The files contain photographs of Mandelstam and Der Nister. In each case (Documents M–6 and K–25), there is a pair of photographs, one profile and one full face. In his photographs, Mandelstam clearly is wearing the leather coat that his wife mentioned in her memoirs. At this point the coat was still in excellent condition. Given the poor heating and high rates of theft in Soviet penal institutions, prisoners were probably most reluctant to take off their coats. Mandelstam's photograph was taken at Butyrka Prison, to which he was transferred four months after his arrest. In the picture, his head is held high and defiant. At some point, the April 30 cover page in his file (Document M–4) was stamped "Photographed." This was probably done upon the taking of the photograph in Document M–6. Der Nister's photograph is accompanied by a crude handwritten note, suggesting that it may have been taken later, perhaps after he arrived at the camp. If it had been taken in Moscow at the Internal Prison of the Ministry of State Security or at Lefortovo Prison, one would have expected a standard form similar to that used for Mandelstam. Perhaps the prison had run out of forms, or perhaps the photograph was added only later at the labor camp. In any event, he looks old and tired, in sharp contrast to Mandelstam's appearance.

■ Permission to Receive Items

The prison authorities appear to have been seriously worried about Der Nister's health. This appears from the medical records discussed below. These same concerns may have prompted them to allow Der Nister's wife to give him warm clothing. A note (Document K–18) dated July 28, 1949, states:

> We report that arrestee KAGANOVICH Pinkhos Mendelevich has been permitted to receive from his wife, SIGALOVSKAIA Elena Klement'evna, residing at: Malaia Bronnaia, 4, Dormitory of the Jewish Theater: worn men's slippers—one pair, a cap, a sweater, warm long underwear—one pair, wool socks—2 pairs, a backpack or suitcase with a lock.

Because of poor or nonexistent heating in prisons and camps, many victims of the Soviet system, when realizing they were being arrested, hastened to put on numerous layers of warm clothing before going away with the arresting officers. Whatever Der Nister put on, his wife was undoubtedly sensible in bringing him additional warm clothing, even in July. This concern for Der Nister's health was not necessarily humanitarian. At the time of Der Nister's arrest, Stalin was playing a complex game, cultivating foreign Jewish opinion by supporting the new state of Israel at the same time as he was crushing Jewish culture in the Soviet Union.[10] It would not have helped this international propaganda campaign if it became known that Der Nister had died soon after his arrest.

■ Prisoner Interrogation Records

As mentioned above, investigation records and personal records were kept separately. The personal records for Mandelstam and Der Nister, which are the subject of this book, do not contain any notes by their interrogators—these would have been in the investigation records. Indeed, Mandelstam's record does not even have any indication that he was interrogated. The Der Nister records, on the other hand, provide a detailed chronicle of when his interrogations took place. Numerous camp memoirs discuss "the conveyor," a method of breaking down prisoners by a combination of intensive questioning and sleep disruption. The records on Der Nister provide an unusually good record of this practice.

Solzhenitsyn writes:

> Sleeplessness was a great form of torture: it left no visible marks and could not provide grounds for complaint. . . . In all the interrogation prisons the prisoners were forbidden to sleep even one minute from reveille till taps. . . . Since the major interrogations were all conducted at night, it was automatic: whoever was undergoing interrogation got no sleep at all for at least five days and nights. (Saturday and Sunday nights, the interrogators themselves tried to get some rest.)[11]

The detailed records of the times of Der Nister's questioning are an artifact of the strict security measures in effect in Lefortovo Prison. Guards signed prisoners out of cells and into questioning rooms and back into their cells. There is, in Kahanovitch's file, what appears to be a complete set of forms from his questioning, fifty-nine forms in all. Nearly all of these forms are similar in content. All show "E. Tsvetaev" as the interrogator. With a few exceptions, indicated in the list below, the only significant difference among the forms is in date and time. Only one of the forms (Document K–85) is reproduced here.

To give an idea of the relentless, often late-night questioning under the "conveyor" system, here are the times shown on the forms:

Monday, February 21, 1949, 2:00 A.M.–4:00 A.M.
Tuesday, February 22, 1949, 11:50 P.M.–4:40 A.M.
Wednesday, February 23, 1949, 11:45 P.M.–4:00 A.M.
Thursday, February 24, 1949, 11:30 P.M.–4:00 A.M.
Friday, February 25, 1949, 3:30 P.M.–5:10 P.M. and 10:50 P.M.
Saturday, February 26, 1949, 1:30 P.M.–4:50 P.M.

Monday, February 28, 1949, 11:10 P.M.–4:00 A.M.
Tuesday, March 1, 1949, 10:30 P.M.–4:20 A.M.

Wednesday, March 2, 1949, 11:50 P.M.–4:00 A.M.
Thursday, March 3, 1949, 11:20 P.M.–5:05 P.M. and
11:15 P.M.–4:00 A.M.
Friday, March 4, 1949, "included in release of [food]
products"
Saturday, March 5, 1949, 1:30 P.M.–5:10 P.M.

Tuesday, March 8, 1949, 11(?):30 P.M.–4:00 A.M.
Thursday, March 10, 1949, 1:20 P.M.–5:05 P.M.
Saturday, March 12, 1949, 1:30 P.M.–4:50 P.M.

Tuesday, March 15, 1949, 11:55 P.M.–4:00 A.M.
Wednesday, March 16, 1949, 1:30 P.M.–5:10 P.M.
Saturday, March 19, 1949, 1:30 P.M.–4:50 P.M.

Monday, March 21, 1949, 1:30 P.M.–5:00 P.M. and
11:50 P.M.–4:00 A.M.
Thursday, March 24, 1949, 1:30 P.M.–5:30 P.M.
Friday, March 25, 1949, 1:20 P.M.–5:10 P.M.

Wednesday, March 30, 1949, 1:30 P.M.–5:10 P.M.

Monday, April 4, 1949, 1:30 P.M.–3:30 P.M.
Wednesday, April 6, 1949, 1:20 P.M.–5:00 P.M.
Thursday, April 7, 1949, 1:30 P.M.–5:00 P.M.
Friday, April 8, 1949, 1:30 P.M.–5:10 P.M.
Saturday, April 9, 1949, 1:30 P.M.–5:10 P.M.

Tuesday, April 12, 1949, 1:30 P.M.–5:00 P.M.
Wednesday, April 13, 1949, 1:30 P.M.–5:20 P.M.
Thursday, April 14, 1949, 1:20 P.M.–5:00 P.M.

Monday, April 18, 1949, 1:30 P.M.–5:00 P.M.
Tuesday, April 19, 1949, 1:20 P.M.–5:00 P.M.
Thursday, April 21, 1949, 1:30 P.M.–5:10 P.M.

Tuesday, April 26, 1949, 1:20 P.M.–5:00 P.M.

Wednesday, April 27, 1949, 1:30 P.M.–5:00 P.M.
Tuesday, May 3, 1949, 1:30 P.M.–3:00 P.M.
Thursday, May 5, 1949, 1:35 P.M.–5:00 P.M.

Thursday, May 12, 1949, 1:20 P.M.–5:00 P.M.

Tuesday, May 24, 1949, 1:30 P.M.–5:30 P.M.

Wednesday, June 15, 1949, 1:25 P.M.–2:40 P.M.
Wednesday, June 15, 1949, 3:30 P.M.–5:10 P.M.
Wednesday, June 15, "returned to cell 134 after
   questioning"
Friday, June 17, 1949, 1:20 P.M.–5:10 P.M.

Tuesday, June 21, 1949, 1:20 P.M.–2:40 P.M.

Tuesday, June 28, 1949, 1:30 P.M.–5:10 P.M.
Thursday, June 30, 1949, 3:40 P.M.–5:15 P.M.

Thursday, July 14, 1949, 2:40 P.M.–5:20 P.M.

Wednesday, July 20, "returned to cell 134"
Thursday, July 21, 1949, 1:30 P.M.–4:20 P.M.
Friday, July 22, 1949, 1:30 P.M.–4:40 P.M.
Thursday, July 28, 1949, 1:30 P.M.–5:10 P.M.
Friday, July 29, 1949, 1:30 P.M.–5:20 P.M.

Saturday, August 6, 1949, 1:30 P.M.–4:30 P.M.

Monday, August 8, 1949, 4:00 P.M.–5:20 P.M.
Tuesday, August 9, 1949, 11:50 P.M.–1:30 A.M.
Wednesday, August 10, 1949, 1:15 P.M.–2:35 P.M.
Wednesday, August 10, 1949, 11:24 P.M.–12:35 A.M.
Thursday, August 11, 1949, "returned to cell 134
   after questioning"

Monday, August 15, 1949, 3:10 P.M.–5:10 P.M. and
   11:40 P.M.–3:30 A.M.

Friday, August 19, 1949, 11:40 P.M.–1:40 A.M.

Tuesday, October 11, 1949, "transferred to cell 121."

■ Extension of Detention

Judging from Der Nister's record, it appears to have been the practice of the Ministry of State Security to require formal monthly extensions of the period of detention. On four separate occasions, the Head of the First Division of Department "A" of the Ministry of State Security issued orders to extend the detention (*soderzhanie pod strazhei*) of Kahanovitch. The first order (Document K–12) is dated April 16, 1949, recorded April 19, 1949, and calls for an extension of detention until May 19, 1949. The second (Document K–13) is dated May 18, 1949, recorded May 20, 1949, and calls for an extension until June 19, 1949. The third (Document K–19) is dated June 15, 1949, recorded June 16, 1949, and calls for an extension until July 19, 1949. The fourth (Document K–16) is dated July 15, 1949, recorded July 16, 1949, and calls for an extension until August 19, 1949. Der Nister was being held under the unpublished rules of the Special Board rather than the rules of the Criminal Procedure Code. However, it is clear that these unpublished rules were modeled to a considerable extent upon those of the Criminal Procedure Code. This Code operated on the principle of one-month extensions of the pretrial process:

> The conduct of inquiry may not extend for more than one month, including in that time also the act of submission to the court. Extension of this period is allowed in the manner established by Art. 116. . . . (Criminal Procedure Code, Art. 105)
>
> Preliminary investigation in cases of crimes listed in Art. 108 must be completed in a two-month period from the start of this investigation, including in this period also the formal transfer to the court or the termination of criminal prosecution. Extension of this period, as well as of the period for the making of inquiry (Art. 105) in individual cases, is allowed only for a period not over one month

with the permission of the provincial (or regional) procurator by a ruling by him giving a reason. The right for further extension of the term for an individual case and also for a general extension of periods for individual districts of the republic where such an extension is required by local conditions belongs to the Procurator of the Republic. (Criminal Procedure Code, Art. 116)

The prisoner awaiting a "trial" by the Special Board was in a worse position than the ordinary prisoner in two respects. First, the decision to extend the investigation appears to have been made by the investigator alone, without a requirement of permission from an appropriate procurator. Second, no reason appears to have been required.

Der Nister remained in Lefortovo Prison beyond the August 19, 1949, date specified by the last extension-of-detention form in the file. Probably formal detention-extension forms were required only during the period of inquiry. The period of inquiry in fact ended on August 17, with the investigator's conclusion that Der Nister was guilty and should be sent to a special camp.

■ The Decision to Send to a Special Camp

The Special Camps (*Osobye lageria*) were instituted in the late 1940s. They were designed to isolate political prisoners and to subject them to a particularly harsh living and working regime combined with political reeducation.[12] The combination of high work norms and low food allowances in the Special Camps made a sentence to them, for many prisoners, a sentence to death by slow starvation. For prisoners such as Kahanovitch with serious preexisting health problems, the sentence to a special camp was a sentence to a relatively rapid death.

The investigator's decision to send Der Nister to a "Special Camp" (Document K–23) came over a month *before* he was convicted by the Special Board. This decision was made not by a court, not even by the Special Board, but by the investigator assigned to his case. It is reported in a formal "DECISION" by the investigator, Lieutenant Colonel Tsvetaev, dated August 17, 1949, and with an unsigned indication of approval by the investigator's superior, Colonel Komarov. Investigator Tsvetaev stated in this document that the investigation had established that "KAHANOVITCH over a period of years had conducted hostile nationalistic activity and in his criminal work was connected with especially dangerous state criminals." He therefore made a decision (*postanovil*) that Kahanovitch be sent to a "special camp" of the Ministry of Internal Affairs. The copy of the decision to send to a special camp in Kahanovitch's record appears to be a carbon copy. Presumably the original was kept in the files of the Ministry of State Security.

The existence or nonexistence of a "presumption of innocence" under Soviet law has been a subject of debate among American specialists in Soviet law and among Soviet legal writers themselves.[13] This order shows that in political cases under Stalin there was a presumption of guilt, not a presumption of innocence.

◼ The Decision of the Special Board

The Special Board (*Osoboe Soveshchanie*) was the successor to a long line of Soviet and czarist administrative bodies with the arbitrary power to order imprisonment.[14] The Special Board that convicted Mandelstam and Der Nister was created by a resolution of November 5, 1934 (SZ SSSR, 1935, No. 11, item 84). This resolution created a Special Board consisting of the Deputy People's Commissars of Internal Affairs, the Agent of the USSR Commissariat of People's Commissars for the RSFSR, the Head of the Main Administration of the Workers' and Peasants' Militia (the police), and the People's Commissar of Internal Affairs of the union republic upon whose territory the case arose. The resolution gave the Special Board the power to impose sentences upon "persons recognized as especially dangerous." Nothing in the resolution required a finding that the person sentenced had committed any particular crime. The most severe authorized sentence was five years in a labor camp. By Der Nister's time, the Special Board had been moved to the newly created Ministry of State Security. Secret decrees had given it the power to impose longer sentences.

The "Excerpt from the Record" of the Special Board (Document M–3) ordered:

> MANDEL´SHTAM Osip Emil´evich is to be confined to a correctional labor camp for counterrevolutionary activity for a term of FIVE years. . . .

It did not cite a specific article of the Criminal Code. As mentioned above, the Special Board could sentence anyone whom it found to be "especially dangerous" whether or not the person had committed a crime. The fact that the signature of "I. Shapiro," the "Responsible Secretary of the Special Board," was stamped rather than handwritten suggests that the issuance of Special Board decisions was a high-volume operation. The record bears the number "77," very likely meaning that this was the seventy-seventh case of the day's session—Rossi reports 600 cases (including his own) being heard in one day in April 1939.[15] There is also a case number, "19390/ts." At the bottom of the "Excerpt from the Record" is the legend "*T[ipografiia]. im[eni]. Vorovskogo. N.* 13015" (Vorovskii Press, No. 13015). This appears to be the name of the organization that printed this form. It might be interesting to try to track the records of this organization, since knowing the number of forms printed would give some idea of the volume of operations of the Special Board. The excerpt from the record also indicates "File is to be deposited in the archive." This would be the report of the interrogation and other evidence that established Mandelstam's "guilt." As indicated above, this file was separate from Mandelstam's personal detention file.

The Mandelstam sentence is for "FIVE years, calculating the term from April 30, 1938." Apparently the Special Board followed a procedure similar to that required by the Criminal Code, Article 29 of which required the subtraction of presentence detention time from the sentence: "The period of preliminary confinement . . . must be counted in the term of deprivation of freedom determined by the court."

Mandelstam was, in fact, not detained until May 2, 1938. Thus he received credit for three extra days. The reason was not a burst of leniency by the tribunal that was sending him to his death. It probably was the lack of any document in the file indicating the date when Mandelstam was actually detained. Every file for a person who had been detained would have an "order to receive" the arrestee (on a coupon attached to the arrest warrant). (In the Stalinist bureaucratic police state, detentions were arbitrary from the point of view of the prisoner, but not from the point of view of the prison, which undoubtedly would refuse to receive anyone without a written order to receive.) So it was most likely the practice of the Special Board just to use the date of the order to receive. Given the fact that a very high percentage of prisoners died during their assigned term and that terms of imprisonment were arbitrarily extended for many of the survivors, there was no reason to worry much about a few days.

By the time Der Nister was sentenced, the Special Board had been transferred to the newly created USSR Ministry of State Security. The maximum sentence that the board could impose had been lengthened. In Der Nister's case, the board was presented with an allegation of a violation of specific articles of the RSFSR Criminal Code, namely Article 58–10, part 1, and Article 58–11. These articles provided the following:

58–10. Propaganda or agitation containing a call for the overthrow, undermining, or weakening of Soviet power or for the commission of individual counterrevolutionary crimes (Articles 58–2–58–9 of the present Code), and also the distribution or preparation or keeping of literature of the same content shall entail:

—deprivation of freedom for a term of not less than six months.

The same acts in the event of mass disturbances or with the use of religious or national prejudices of the masses or in a war situation, or in places declared to be on war status shall entail:

—the measures of social defense indicated in Article 58–2 of the present Code.

58–11. Every type of organizational activity directed at the preparation or commission of the crimes defined in the present Chapter and also participation in an organization formed for the preparation or commission of one of the crimes defined in the present Chapter shall entail:

—the measures of social defense indicated in the corresponding articles of the present Chapter.

The board sentenced Der Nister (Document K–21) under Articles 58–10, pt. 1, and 58–11 "for criminal ties with nationalists and for anti-Soviet agitation" to ten years, "calculating the term from February 19, 1949." Unlike Mandelstam, who was merely found guilty of "counterrevolutionary activity" in general, Der Nister was found guilty of violating specific articles of the Code. In this respect, as in others, Der Nister's file reflects procedures closer to those in ordinary criminal cases. However, this shift is also a shift away from the honesty of the pre–World War II Soviet extraordinary tribunals, which were blatantly arbitrary.

■ The Prisoner's Acknowledgment of Receipt of the Decision of the Special Board

On the back of the "Extract from the Protocol of the Special Board" that sentenced Mandelstam is stamped: "The ruling of the special board has been read by _____." Mandelstam's signature is on the line provided. Beneath his signature is the handwritten word "Notified" (*Ob''iavleno*), the date 8/8–38, and an illegible signature. In a regular trial, the sentence would be read aloud to all those present in the courtroom, including the defendant (Art. 339 of the 1923 Criminal Procedure Code). One theoretical purpose was to start the rehabilitation process by informing the defendant of the crime he was found to have committed and the punishment he would receive. Since the person whose case was being considered by the Special Board—not really a "defendant," since he had no chance to defend himself—was not present at the meeting of the Special Board where the sentence was imposed, this purpose could be accomplished only by a later presentation of a summary of the action of the Special Board to the person sentenced.

The handwritten statement in this case served the purpose of providing a date for the record of the time when the Special Board's sentence was shown to Mandelstam. In some cases, the person sentenced would refuse to sign. Then the notation that the sentence had been presented to him would operate as a substitute for the signature. As with the other documents, Mandelstam's signature is in a strong hand.

■ Notice

Physically sewn to the coupon of the arrest warrant is a "Notice" (Document K–1) stamped with the date October 6, 1949, indicating that "after sentencing" Kahanovitch is to be sent to a "SPECIAL camp." "For persons convicted by the Special Board, the orders [for transfer to a special camp or special prison] arrive at the prison together with extracts from the decisions of the Special Board." Such an order for transfer to a special camp is indeed included in Der Nister's file and is discussed below. Although this particular notice is stamped with a date later than the date of Der Nister's conviction, the language of the notice form suggests that it is designed to be attached to the prisoner's record even before conviction. This further confirms the absence of any presumption of innocence.

■ Transfer to Being Held for the Special Board

An order in Der Nister's file, dated October 5, 1949, and entered into the file the next day (Document K–20), indicates that he is being reassigned as a prisoner being held for the Special Board. This order seems to have been issued somewhat late, because it appears to be designed for use at the time the file goes to the Special Board for consideration rather than after conviction.

■ Order to Transfer to a Labor Camp

There is a formal document on transfer to a labor camp in Der Nister's file, but not in Mandelstam's. Less than a week after being transferred to the jurisdiction of the Special Board attached to the Ministry of State Security, Der Nister was transferred to the jurisdiction of the "Special Department" of the Second Administration of the Main Administration of Correctional Labor Camps and Colonies ("GULAG") of the Ministry of Internal Affairs, which was responsible for administering the labor camps. At this point he moved to the jurisdiction of a different ministry. This "Special Department"—the department for political prisoners—issued an "Order" (Document K–22) dated October 14, 1949, which provided the basis for sending Der Nister to a specific labor camp. The absence of such a document from Mandelstam's file is rather surprising, since generally prisoner transfers must have been carefully documented to avoid "leakage" in the system. Most likely Mandelstam was part of a group transfer of prisoners under a single order, so that there was no individual order to put in his file.

A "Certificate" in the file (Document K–26), signed by the Head of Lefortovo Prison, Lieutenant Ionov, cites the MVD order of October 14 mentioned above (Document K–22) and also cites an MGB order of October 15, which is not in the file. This document repeats the basic facts about Kahanovitch and his assignment to the Mineral'nyi Camp. A physician has signed to the effect that Der Nister is "Healthy, may travel," and has "Passed physical exam." The document also indicates, "There were no epidemic illnesses in the prison." Obviously Der Nister was not healthy, since the doctors who had seen him had correctly diagnosed the illnesses that were to progress and prove fatal. But the authorities were probably worried mainly about contagious diseases. The death of a prisoner in transit would be no particular problem. However, one that infected other prisoners might reduce the supply of labor badly needed by the camps to meet their plan.

In assigning a sentenced political prisoner to a camp, the department had to consider the kind of camp designated by the Ministry of State Security, in Der Nister's case a "Special Camp." Other factors it might have taken into account would include the ability of camps to accept extra prisoners and the need of camps for extra labor to fulfill their production plans.

The October 14 order states that Der Nister is "fit for light physical work" and that his specialty is "writer." The Special Department may have taken Der Nister's poor health and lack of craft skills into account in the selection of a particular camp. Inmate skills and physical abilities were reevaluated by the camps on arrival—this evaluation will be discussed below.

■ Camp Records—Form No. 1

A "Form No. 1—Statistical-Record Card" was filled out for Mandelstam upon his arrival at the camp on October 12, 1938. This is in his file as Documents M–2 and M–2BACK. (There is another, virtually identical copy of the same document in his file, Document M–16.) The top of the form is filled out in purple ink in a neat handwriting; the remainder of the form is filled out in a less legible, more cursive handwriting in blue ink; the form is signed by Mandelstam in the same blue ink. What probably happened was that a few key questions were filled out as arriving prisoners were processed; the remaining questions were then answered later on the basis of documents in the prisoner's file. These key items included the file number of the record, his category of fitness for work, his name, his date of birth, and his social origin. The most important thing a camp administration needed to decide upon the arrival of a prisoner was his work assignment. Typically a "commission" examined each arriving prisoner.[16]

Mandelstam was classified as suitable for "medium" physical labor. This classification had two effects, at least in theory: first, it might determine the type of labor to which a prisoner was assigned, and second, it would determine the amount of piecework the prisoner had to do to obtain a full food allowance.[17] The food-allowance system was the key to camp discipline and most likely was an important contributing cause to Mandelstam's death. The basic food allowance was barely enough to sustain life. If a prisoner did not fulfill the piecework plan for someone of his category (in Mandelstam's case, "medium physical labor"), he got a reduced food allowance, which was a sentence to death by slow starvation. Reclassification of prisoners to lower categories of fitness for work (and hence to lower piecework norms to obtain full food rations) generally lagged behind the actual deterioration of the prisoner's health. So once a prisoner began to weaken and his piecework output fell, he would receive smaller food rations, in a vicious cycle that would end with his death from lack of food.

The back of Form No. 1 (Document M–2BACK) has blanks for keeping track of the prisoner's work record. But in Mandelstam's file, none of the blanks are filled in.

Kahanovitch's camp record data card (Documents K–27/28) is dated December 9, 1949, and lists him as having arrived on December 1, 1949. The form used was still called "Form No. 1," but it was a substantially improved version of the "Form No. 1" used in Mandelstam's time. It provided much more room for information related to the basic purpose of labor camps—labor. Although in the order sending him to camp Kahanovitch was classified as fit for "light physical labor," within a month and a half after arriving at the camp, on January 21, 1950, he was reclassified as "disabled." This classification was reconfirmed on February 19, 1950, and May 7, 1950. The February 19 and May 7 classifications contain a reference to "Section 24," presumably a section of the guidelines on classification with regard to fitness for work.

The form has seven sections: I, information on the prisoner and his sentence; II, distinguishing features; III, "Notes on movement"; IV, Changes of the term of punishment); V, Penalties and awards; VI, (Conclusions of the skill-evaluation commission; and VII, Results of medical examinations. During the 1940s there was a gradual convergence of the conditions of "free" labor and camp labor. "Free" workers were forbidden to quit their jobs without permission. They were subject to severe punishment for tardiness and other offenses but could obtain rewards for exemplary performance. Wages were low; piecework bonuses were essential to making a living wage. Wages and assignments were based upon the skill qualifications formally assigned to each worker. All these conditions applied also to camp inmates, except that food allowances largely took the place of wages. Each "free" worker had a labor booklet (*Trudovaia knizhka* in Russian), which contained his or her name, age, education, skill, work history, transfer, causes of transfer, and rewards and awards. This booklet was kept in the personnel office of the worker's employer. By the time Der Nister reached his labor camp, Form No. 1 had come to resemble the labor booklet in many ways.

■ Certification on Property

A note dated February 27, 1950 (Document K–24) states, "prisoners [illegible] Volkov Pavel Iakovlevich and Kaganovich /Der Nister/ Pinkhas Mendelevich were convicted by a sentence without confiscation of property." Perhaps these prisoners succeeded in bringing some belongings to the camp, and the question then arose as to whether these belongings should have been confiscated. The memo in the file is a copy of a reply to an inquiry of February 23, 1950. It is directed to the head of the "Special Section" (*spetschast'*) in Abez', where the camp was located, and is signed by a "Senior Inspector of the Special Department." The note indicates that it was made in two copies, one to "adm." and one to the file.

The significance of this document is what it tells us about the structure and communications of the system for dealing with political prisoners. Although the Ministry of State Security turned political prisoners over to the Ministry of Internal Affairs, there was an administrative linkage running from the Ministry of State Security through the Special Department of the Second Main

Administration of the Ministry of Internal Affairs to "special sections" in the individual camps. In discussions in Moscow in 1994 with a private business manager, I learned that the Ministry of Internal Affairs was marketing to selected business clients the use of its internal courier service, which, I was told, had functioned for years to transfer communications between the ministry in Moscow and various organizations subordinate to it. Quite probably this courier service was in operation in 1950 and was used both for the inquiry about confiscation and for the reply. Since the reply is labeled "secret," it is unlikely it was sent through the regular mail or other insecure channels.

■ Medical Treatment

Millions of inmates died due to the poor conditions of life in the camps. The camps were unsanitary and overcrowded. The amount of food was deliberately kept low in quantity and quality, so that the slow starvation of the less productive workers would provide an object lesson for shirkers. Der Nister had a serious preexisting medical condition, which manifested itself almost immediately after his arrest (Documents K–7 and K–10). Mandelstam's arrest picture suggests that he had, until his arrest, enjoyed somewhat too much of the classic Russian high-fat, high-cholesterol diet. Der Nister was around 66 years old; Mandelstam was 47. The harsh conditions in the camps, however, claimed many younger and healthier victims.

Nadezhda Mandelstam's memoirs give no hint that Osip Mandelstam had any serious health problems in the months immediately preceding his arrest. Mandelstam himself looks basically healthy in his arrest photograph; his signature on documents dating from the first months after his arrest is firm and sure. There are only two fragmentary items in the record indicating that Mandelstam was given some medical attention on the last day of his life. A handwritten "Certificate" (Document M–9) dated December 27 states "Prisoner Mendel´shtam was under treatment since December 26 died December 27 at 12:30."

A typewritten death certificate (Document M–11) dated December 27, 1938 states that Mandelstam was placed in an infirmary (*statsionar*) on December 26, 1938. However, there is no record of any treatment being administered.

There are many villains and few decent people in these records. One Ianshin, on July 4, 1949, wrote a request (Document K–14) for medical treatment for Kahanovitch. It is hard to say whether Ianshin felt sympathy for Kahanovitch or merely wanted to avoid the embarrassment of having a prisoner die under his care. Ianshin was a lieutenant colonel in the Medical Service and served as head of the Health Section of Lefortovo Prison. According to Ianshin's diagnosis, Kahanovitch suffered from severely bleeding hemorrhoids, to the point where loss of blood was "very dangerous." Ianshin wrote "Conservative methods of treatment are not giving adequate results." (The Russian text says *"ne daiut dostatochnykh rezul'tatom,"* evidently a typographical error for *"rezul'tatov."*) He went on to recommend, "Prisoner KAGANOVICH must be shown to a qualified surgeon for consultation and the possibility of treatment by an operation." A cover sheet on this medical report (Document K–15) was addressed to Major General Comrade Leonov, the head of the Investigation Department for Especially Important Cases.

Ianshin's suggestion was taken. The next item in the file (Document K–17) is dated July 20 and states:

> Prisoner Kaganovitch, P.M., on July 20, 1949, was examined by a surgical specialist attached to the hospital of Butyrka Prison of the MVD, Lieutenant Colonel of the Medical Service Comrade Finaev, to the effect that at the present time the prisoner, with respect to his hemorrhoids, does not need operative intervention. Conservative treatment has been prescribed.

Der Nister received extensive though unsuccessful medical treatment. His file contains about forty pages of records (e.g., Document K–32) from the Central Hospital at the Mineral'nyi Labor Camp. They appear to reflect serious, professional medical treatment. He may have had the luck to have had some first-class physicians as fellow inmates.

■ Death Certificates

> In June 1940, M[andelstam]'s brother Alexander was summoned to the Registry Office of the Bauman district and handed M.'s death certificate with instructions to pass it on to me. M's age was given as forty-seven, and the date of his death as December 27, 1938. The cause was given as "heart failure." This is as much as to say that he died because he died: what is death but heart failure? There was also something about arteriosclerosis.[18]

Camp record-keeping rules required the completion of a formal death certificate for each prisoner who died. Mandelstam's death certificate (Document M–11) is typed as a whole—it does not appear to be a form whose blanks were filled in later. The cause of death "Stoppage of the heart arteriocerebrosclerosis" corresponds to that mentioned by Nadezhda Mandelstam in her memoirs, quoted above. Nadezhda Mandelstam and others have raised questions about the truth of this statement.[19] The statement on the death certificate that there was no autopsy does not help to solve these doubts. Der Nister's death certificate (Document K–29) reflects the apparent lack or shortage of typewriters in the camp where he was. It is a handwritten standard form, presumably prepared by an inmate scribe, with details filled out in another hand. Given the deteriorating condition shown in the extensive medical records, there is little reason to doubt the cause of death shown.

■ Postmortem Fingerprinting

Fingerprinting was used to authenticate the identity of prisoners who died in the camps. A fundamental requirement of any system of prison administration is keeping careful records of the inmate population. If supervisors could not check the inmate population, there would always be the possibility that local camp administrators would cover up cases in which prisoners had escaped or, even worse, would take bribes to allow escapes that they would then cover up. Since missing prisoners would not be present to answer roll calls, the only acceptable excuses for the absence of a prisoner would be that he had been formally checked out of the camp to another destination or had died. Supervision of camps required evidence beyond a mere death certificate. This was provided by a procedure for taking postmortem fingerprints, having a fingerprint expert compare them with the fingerprints in the prisoner's file, and having this expert certify their identity.

The Mandelstam file shows how this system worked. Document M–8 has the fingerprints taken on May 14, 1938, at the Internal Prison of the Main Administration of State Security, where Mandelstam was first held. Looking at this form, we see that the fingerprints show the hands of a writer, not a manual laborer. The prints are clear and sharp, reflecting the high technical quality of the Moscow state security apparatus. The Internal Prison also has enough volume and enough resources to have secured a stamp with its name to put on the standard fingerprint forms. The postmortem fingerprints (Document M–10) are technically of slightly worse quality. The inking appears to have been inferior. The camp fingerprint office lacked a rubber stamp with its name. However, there are serious lines and scars on a number of the fingers. The fact that the same white spaces appear on both the basic and the check sets of fingerprints shows that these are scars and not merely artifacts of bad inking. In comparing the two sets of prints, note that, for the right hand, the little finger is on the right in both sets of prints; but for the left hand, the little finger is on the right in the basic set and on the left in the check set. The lines and scars must reflect injury to the fingers due to the harsh life in the camps and possibly also some postmortem changes in the fingers.

Each set of fingerprints is appropriately authenticated. The first set of fingerprints is authenticated by Mandelstam's unmistakable signature, witnessed by a prison officer. As in the other documents signed soon after the arrest, the hand is firm and sure. The postmortem set obviously has no such signature. Instead it is authenticated by a "Record of Identity." This Record of Identity (Document M–7) consists of handwritten entries on a typewritten form. The typewriting is a somewhat blurred and faded blue. Like the *samizdat* of the Khrushchev and Brezhnev eras, it appears to be one of multiple carbon copies made on a typewriter. The typed year is given as "193," with a blank. The protocol was filled out, in fact, on December 31, 1938. Probably toward the end of the year 1938, the typist produced forms with the last digit of the year blank, so that any leftovers could be used in 1939. Unfortunately, the form has no serial number that could be used as a basis for estimating the number of postmortem fingerprint analyses done at this camp in 1938.

The expert certifies that both fingerprints are identical and that both have the same numerical classification code in the system used in Soviet criminalistics of the time.

■ Burial

There is no burial certificate in the files for Mandelstam, but there is one for Der Nister (Document K–30). Like the death certificates, the burial certificates were handwritten in one color ink and filled out in another. Obviously some inmate was employed to handwrite a supply of death certificates in advance of the inevitable need for them. The burial procedures were standardized, since they are described in the standard form part of the certificate. Prisoners were buried in underclothing (or nothing at all), outergarments (and sometimes even undergarments) being in short supply in the camps. The certificate lists the names of two witnesses to the burial, one from the Guard Service and one from the Central Hospital. The name of the guard-service witness is part of the form document, while the name of the hospital witness is written in later.

If the certificate can be believed, Der Nister got a much more decent burial than most of his cohort. There was a wooden coffin, a tag with his name on his leg, and a stake with an identifying code. One would like to think that these features of the burial represented a small touch of humanity. They did create some possibility for future generations in a more free society to identify at least some of the bodies of victims of the GULAG and to give them proper burials with appropriate ceremonies. However, the careful identification of the corpse may have had a more practical purpose. A faked death could have been the best way to escape from a camp; it certainly would be the best way for camp authorities to cover up having allowed an escape to occur. If a prisoner failed to show up for roll call, a huge hunt and chase would have ensued because of the draconian penalties imposed on camp administrators who allowed escapes to occur. However, if a prisoner were duly certified as dead, there would be no further investigation. If bodies were dumped into a common grave or were burned, postmortem audits of death certificates would be difficult or impossible. The practice of carefully identifying the corpse made easy any subsequent exhumation for audit. Writing of the prewar period, Solzhenitsyn discussed a progression from burial in ordinary underwear, to burial in low-grade underwear, to burial naked. He also mentioned the rarity of coffins and grave markers.[20]

If an escapee were caught or an exhumation revealed an empty grave, those who had signed the burial certificate would face severe punishment. By requiring multiple signatures on a burial certificate, the authorities could make it more difficult for prisoners to bribe camp authorities or for camp authorities to fake deaths to cover up escapes. (Game theory suggests that bribing several people is much more difficult than bribing one, because each prospective bribe recipient must fear that one of the others will turn him in, and this fear will lead each, if he accepts a bribe at all, to demand a bribe higher than one single person would have asked, as compensation for the higher risk.) The certificate had places for three signatures, for representatives of (1) the Guard Service, (2) the Special Section, and (3) the hospital. This certificate is signed only by representatives of the Guard Service and the hospital. Either procedures were somewhat lax, or signature by representatives of the Special Section was only required in certain situations, of which this was not one.

■ Correspondence with Relatives

In her memoir, Nadezhda Mandelstam reports that in early 1939 she was informed by a postal clerk that a mailing sent to her husband had been returned because "The addressee is dead."[21] There is a letter from Nadezhda Mandelstam in the file (Document M–12), dated February 7, 1939. In it she writes to the Main Administration of Labor Camps, reporting that a "money transfer" to her husband was returned "because of the death of the addressee" and asks for verification of the date of the death. There is a discrepancy between the English-language version of her memoir, which refers to a "parcel," and the letter, which refers to a money transfer (in Russian, *denezhnyi perevod*). In her original Russian memoir, Nadezhda Mandelstam uses the word *posylka*, which normally means "parcel" but may mean merely a "mailing."[22] Most likely the problem is ambiguity of language or ambiguity of memory. Possibly, however, after the package was returned, Nadezhda Mandelstam sent a money transfer to see if it too would be returned. Sending money transfers was a common way to communicate with prisoners.[23] Paradoxically, given the lawless nature of the Soviet state, money-transfer rules were rather well enforced in order to prevent theft.

The body of the letter is written in black ink; the postscript regarding the address is in purple ink. Both are in Nadezhda Mandelstam's very clear handwriting. The paper is lined and appears to have been torn from a binding on the left.

Nadezhda Mandelstam's letter, dated February 7, 1939, is stamped with the date of receipt, written in as February 9, 1939. Although the stamp is poorly legible, it appears to be that of the Inspectorate Attached to the Main Administration of Camps (the infamous "GULAG") of the NKVD. Above the stamp are the initials "URO" ("Accounting Assignment Department") in what appears to be the same hand as the dates written in the stamp. It appears that the letter eventually made its way to Magadan. (Perhaps through the same NKVD courier service mentioned above.) It appears that the camp administration sent the notice both to the civil registry office in Magadan and that in Moscow.

In the top left corner is a light purple stamp saying "Inspectorate attached to the Head of the Main Administration of Camps of the People's Commissariat of Internal Affairs." This is dated February 9, 1939, in ink. It appears to be a stamp placed upon receipt of the document.

Probably the next action after delivery was to determine how this request should be routed. Markings indicate the responsible department, the responsible camp administration, and the serial number of the file. The name "Mandel'shtam Osip Emil'evich" is underlined in red pencil, and the words "1st Department" are written with the same pencil obliquely across the top left corner. The abbreviation of the name of the camp administration is underlined in brown pencil, and the abbreviation is written in brown letters obliquely across the left corner. A poorly legible word, probably "Zek" (prisoner), is written in ordinary pencil in the top left corner. Mandelstam's file number "3/2844" is written in ordinary pencil in the left margin of the letter with a blue circle around it. This version of the number is missing the initial letter "V." Someone started to write the full file number in purple ink but made a mistake, writing "V/." This false start is crossed out and next to it is written the correct file number: "V3/2844." Finally, in the top right corner is the number "1.2." This is a document number, similar to the number on each document in the file. It was probably added much later, perhaps even in the 1990s when the file was photographed. A stamp with the initials "URO" (see above) is on the back of the letter; this may have been stamped by a receiving agency.

There are three documents in the record whose creation was triggered by the letter. The first document (M–14) is a memorandum dated June 26, 1939, stating that Osip Mandelstam died in Vladivostok on December 27, 1938. The second document (M–13) is a standard-form communication dated July 20, 1939, indicating that it is being sent to the Civil Registry in Magadan with the correspondence of relatives about Mandelstam's death. The third document (M–15) is on the same standard form but is addressed to the Civil Registry in Moscow. Some background is necessary to understand these documents. In each Soviet city in the 1930s, there was a Department of Civil Status Registration subordinate to the local office of the People's Commissariat of Internal Affairs. This department was responsible for the registration of births, marriages, and deaths. (Similar offices exist in today's Russia.) In Moscow the Department of Certificates of Civil Status Registration was subordinate to the Moscow city division of the Ministry of Internal Affairs. In Magadan, however, the situation was different, because the administration of Magadan was not organized like that of ordinary Soviet cities; rather, Magadan was run as a colonial outpost by Dal'stroi, the division of the People's Commissariat of Internal Affairs responsible for construction work in the Soviet Far East. (*Dal'* means "far" in Russian; *stroi* means "Construction." Most English speakers think of everything from the Ural Mountains to the Pacific Ocean as "Siberia." Russian speakers, however, distinguish Siberia and the "Far East," the latter being the easternmost provinces of Russia.) An additional clue to what occurred is from Nadezhda Mandelstam's memoirs, in which she writes that her brother received a notice from the Moscow Civil Status Registry indicating that Osip Mandelstam's death had been entered in the registry in 1940.[24]

Quite likely what happened was this. At some time during the first half of 1939 the letter written by Nadezhda Mandelstam to "GULAG" was sent directly or indirectly to the administrative center for the Far Eastern camps, the "Administrative and Recordkeeping Department of the Administration of Northeastern Correctional Labor Camps of the People's Commissariat of Internal Affairs." ("URO USVITL NKVD"). Possibly two inquiries reached it, one directly from Moscow and one from Magadan. It checked Mandelstam's file and found that it indicated that he had died on December 27. The person who checked the files wrote the memorandum of June 26. On the basis of this memorandum, the Administration and Recordkeeping Department replied to both Magadan and Moscow with word of Osip Mandelstam's death. Eventually these replies provided a basis for the action of the Moscow registry. Nadezhda Mandelstam correctly notes that few survivors got information of the death of their loved ones. However, the existence of these printed forms shows that a procedure existed for handling inquiries. What they cannot tell is the percent of inquiries that were actually answered.

CONCLUDING THOUGHTS

Osip Mandelstam and Pinchas Kahanovitch were only two victims of the Soviet labor-camp system. Similar files still exist for millions of others. Further study of these files can help bring a better understanding of the working of this system. For instance, a researcher could trace the formalization of bureaucratic routine from the relatively crude records kept in the late 1930s to the much more sophisticated records kept in the 1940s. Most importantly, publication of more information on the labor-camp system can prevent future generations from denying its existence or minimizing its scale. Further study might also help identify numerous villains and a few heroes. Most of those involved in processing these prisoners appeared to have been concerned only with carrying out orders and producing bureaucratically acceptable paperwork. Only the physicians who took a real interest in Der Nister are an exception. An understanding of the camp records system may help others find their way through the records to learn the fate of friends and loved ones.

NOTES

1. Nadezhda Mandelstam, *Hope Against Hope: A Memoir*, trans. Max Hayward (New York: Atheneum, 1972); Russian original: *Vospominaniia* (New York: Chekhov Publishing House, 1970); Nadezhda Mandelstam, *Hope Abandoned*, trans. Max Hayward (New York: Atheneum, 1974); Russian original: *Vtoraia kniga* (Paris: YMCA Press, 1972). For further details on Osip Mandelstam's life and works, see the excellent biography by Jane Gary Harris, *Osip Mandelstam* (Boston: Twayne Publishers, 1988). Some more-recent materials are in *Zhizn' i tvorchestvo O.E. Mandel'shtama: vospominaniia, materialy k biografii, "novye stikhi," kommentarii, issledovaniia*, ed. O.G. Lasunskii et al. (Izd-vo Voronezhskogo universiteta: Voronezh, 1990).

2. Delphine Bechtel, *Der Nister's Work 1907–1929: A Study of a Yiddish Symbolist* (Berne/New York: P. Lang, 1990); Sol Liptzin, *The Maturing of Yiddish Literature* (New York: Jonathan David Publishers, 1970), pp. 88–93.

3. For a detailed history, see Amy Knight, *The KGB; Police and Politics in the Soviet Union* (Boston: Unwin Hyman, 1988). A very valuable reference source is Jacques Rossi, *Spravochnik po GULagu; Istoricheskii slovar' sovetskikh penitentsiarnykh institutov i terminov, sviazannykh s prinuditel'nym trudom* (The Gulag Handbook; A Historical Dictionary of Soviet Penitentiary Institutions and Terms Related to Forced Labor) (London: Overseas Publications Interchange, Ltd, 1987).

4. Gavriel D. Ra'anan, *International Policy Formation in the USSR: Factional "Debates" During the Zhdanovschina* (Hamden, CT: Archon Books, 1983); Liptzin, *The Maturing of Yiddish Literature*, p. 93.

5. Harold J. Berman, *Soviet Criminal Law and Procedure: The RSFSR Codes*, 2nd ed. (Cambridge, MA: Harvard University Press, 1972), pp. 10, 52–53.

6. Liptzin, *The Maturing of Yiddish Literature*, p. 93.

7. Khone Shmeruck, *Hanazir V'Hadgadyo* (Jerusalem: Mosad Bialik, 1963), p. 17, cited in Leonard Wolf, "Introduction," in *The Family Mashber* (New York: Summit Books, 1987), p. 25.

8. Ibid., p. 17.

9. Aleksandr I. Solzhenitsyn, *The Gulag Archipelago 1918–1956: An Experiment in Literary Investigation*, vol. 3, trans. Thomas P. Whitney (New York: Harper & Row, 1978), p. 193.

10. Ra'anan, *International Policy Formation in the USSR.*

11. Aleksandr I. Solzhenitsyn, *The Gulag Archipelago 1918–1956: An Experiment in Literary Investigation*, vol. 1, trans. Thomas P. Whitney (New York: Harper & Row, 1973), pp. 112–13.

12. Rossi, *Spravochnik po GULagu*, p. 377; Aleksandr I. Solzhenitsyn, *The Gulag Archipelago 1918–1956: An Experiment in Literary Investigation*, vol. 2, trans. Thomas P. Whitney (New York: Harper & Row, 1975), pp. 317, 560, 627–28.

13. Harold J. Berman, "The Presumption of Innocence: Another Reply," *American Journal of Comparative Law* 28: 615-23 (1980); George P. Fletcher, "The Ongoing Soviet Debate About the Presumption of Innocence," *Criminal Justice Ethics* 3: 69–75 (1984); John Quigley, "The Soviet Conception of the Presumption of Innocence," *Santa Clara Law Review* 29: 301-29 (1988).

14. Samuel Kucherov, *The Organs of Soviet Administration of Justice: Their History and Operation* (Leiden: E.J. Brill, 1970), pp. 45–77; Richard Pipes, *Russia Under the Old Regime* (New York: Charles Scribner's Sons, 1974), pp. 299–302; Rossi, *Spravochnik po GULagu*, pp. 254–258.

15. Rossi, *Spravochnik po GULagu,* p. 256.

16. Ibid., pp. 163–64, 416–17.

17. Ibid., pp. 169–170; Sylvestre Mora-Pierre Zwierniak, *La Justice Sovietique* (Rome: Maggi-Spinetti, 1945), p. 312.

18. Mandelstam, *Hope Against Hope*, p. 377.

19. Interviews with camp survivors and other important details are found in Pavel Nerler, "'S Gurboi i gurtom . . .': Khronika poslednogo goda zhizni O. E. Mandel'shtama," *Rubezh'*, 1992, No. 1, 226–49; translated as Pavel Markovich Nerler, "En Masse: A Chronicle of the Last Days of Osip Emilevich Mandelshtam," *Manoa* (Special Feature—Russian Far East, Guest Editor Adele Barker), 1994, Vol. 6, no. 1, p. 182; expanded version published as *"S Gurboi i gurtom" . . .: Khronika poslednogo goda zhizni O. E. Mandel'shtama* (Moscow: Radiks, 1994).

20. Solzhenitsyn, vol. 2, p. 222.

21. Mandelstam, *Hope Against Hope*, pp. 376, 388–90.

22. Mandel'shtam, *Vospominaniia*, p. 395 ("posylku"), p. 407 ("posylki").

23. Rossi, *Spravochnik po GULagu*, p. 274.

24. Mandelstam, *Hope Against Hope*, pp. 373, 377, 389–90.

DOCUMENTS

Mandelstam File	**(M–0—M–16)**
Kahanovitch File	**(K–0—K–85)**

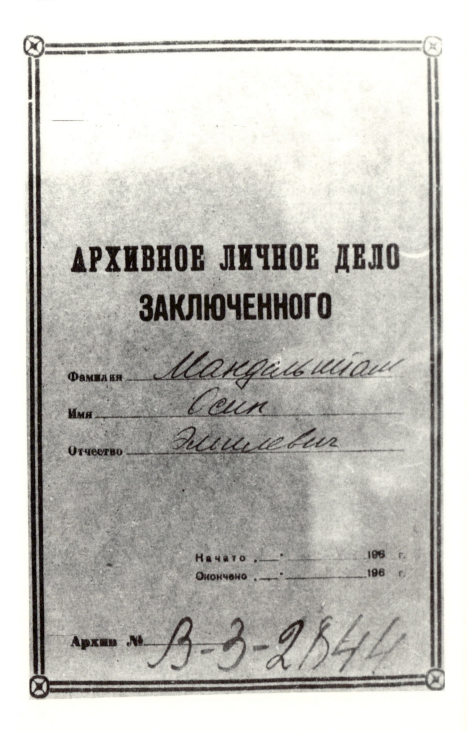

АРХИВНОЕ ЛИЧНОЕ ДЕЛО
ЗАКЛЮЧЕННОГО

Фамилия _Мандельштам_

Имя _Осип_

Отчество _Эмилевич_

Начато ,_'_____ 196_ г.

Окончено ,_'_____ 196_ г.

Архив № _В-3-2Б44_

ARCHIVAL PERSONAL FILE
OF THE PRISONER

Last name _Mandel'shtam_

First name _Osip_

Patronymic _Emilevich_

Begun _____ **196**

Finished _____ **196**

Archive No. _V-3-2844_

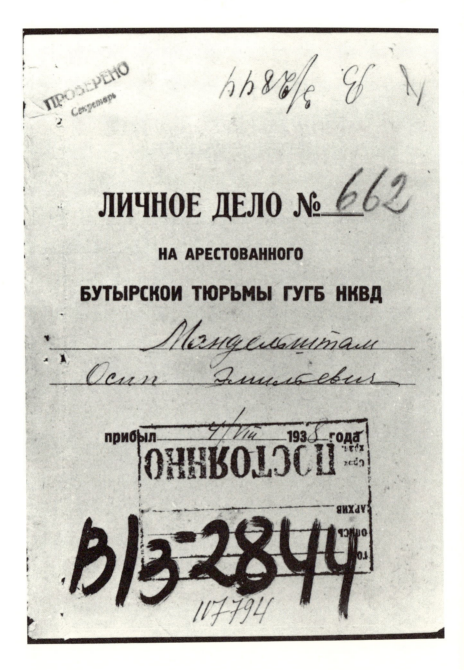

ПРОВЕРЕНО
Секретарь

ЛИЧНОЕ ДЕЛО № 662

НА АРЕСТОВАННОГО

БУТЫРСКОИ ТЮРЬМЫ ГУГБ НКВД

Мендельштам
Осип Эмильевич

прибыл 4/VIII 1938 года

ПОСТОЯННО

В/3-2844

117794

V. 3/2844

CHECKED
Secretary

PERSONAL FILE No. *662*

FOR THE DETAINEE

OF BUTYRKA PRISON
OF THE MAIN ADMINISTRATION
OF THE PEOPLE'S COMMISSARIAT
OF INTERNAL AFFAIRS

Mandel'shtam

Osip Emil'evich

arrived _____ *August 4* _____ **193**_8_

```
|                            |
|YEAR_____    |
|DESCRIPTION_____     |
|ARCHIVE_____     |
|                            |
|TIME TO                     |
|RETAIN PERMANENT            |
```

V/3–2844

117794

Москов 3

форма № 1.

Управление Сев. Восточных Исправительно-Трудовых лагерей Н. К. В. Д.

Учетно-статистическая карточка

Личное дело № _____

Прибыл в лагерь *12 10* 193*8* г.

Место для фотокарточки

Категория содержания				
Категория трудоспособн *Слаб.*				

1. Фамилия и кличка *Мандельштам*
2. Имя и отчество *Осип Эмильевич*
3. Год рожд *1891* Место рождения и приписки *Польша*

ОСОБЫЕ ПРИМЕТЫ

1. Рост *средний*
2. Телосло *худое*
3. Цвет воло *седые*
4. Цвет глаз *карие*
5. Нос *с горбин*
6. Прочие приметы *сгорб*

4. Образование { Общее *Высшее* / Специальное
5. Гражданство *СССР* Национальность *Еврей*
6. Специальность { Общая *писатель и* / Узкая *поэт* / Стаж *29 л*

и пилво пожилых волосами на голове и на виска.

7. Постанов. квалификац. комиссии: _____

8. Какие языки знаете кроме родного *Руг. фр. нем*
9. Социальное происхождение *сын купца*
10. Социальное положение *служащий*
11. Партийность *б/п*

12. Служба в армиях { Старой / Белой / Красной

13. Служба в судебн орган. и НКВД _____
14. Время ареста *3. 05. 1938*
15. Прошлая судимость (который раз в лагере*) *Судим*
16. Семейное положение *женат* указать фамилии и адреса ближних родственников *ж. Надежда Яковл. г. Москва фр.*
17. Постоянное и последнее место жительство *Москва ул 5 № 26 г. Калинин 3 в....*

Отпечаток большого пальца правой руки

Работа до заключения

Учреждение или предприятие	Занимаемая должность	От	До
Жал. литер г. Воронеж	*Лит. работн*	*1934*	*ареста*

Об ответственности за дачу ложных сведений мне объявлено

Подпись заключенного *О. Э. Мандельштам*

Moscow 3   form No. 1.

Administration of Northeast Corrective Labor Camps
of the People's Commissariat of Internal Affairs
Statistical-Record Card

Personal file No. ___

Detention category					Place
Work	*med.phys*				for
category	*labor*				photograph

Arrived at the camp   *Oct. 12*   193*8*

SPECIAL FEATURES

1. Last name and nickname *Mandel'shtam*
2. Name and Patronimic *Osip Emil'evich*
3. Year of birth *1891* Place of birth and of residence permit ___ *Poland*

4. Education { General *Higher*
            { Specialized
5. Citizenship *USSR* Nationality *Jew*
6. Specialty { General *writer and*
            { Narrow *poet*
            { Experience *29 years*

SPECIAL FEATURES
1. Height *Average*
2. Body *Normal*
3. Hair color *Grey*
4. Eye color *Hazel*
5. Nose *hooked*
6. Other features *chest and abdomen covered with hair. Baldness on head*

7. **Ruling of the skill evaluation commission:**

8. What languages do you know beside native? *Rus. Fr. Ger. Ital. Span.*
9. Social origin *son of a merchant*
10. Social position *office worker*
11. Party membership *none*
12. Army Service { Old
                { White
                { Red
13. Service in judicial bodies and People's Comm. of Internal Affairs
14. Time of arrest *May 3, 1938*
15. Prior convictions *convicted art.58* Which time in camp*)
16. Family position *married* indicate name and address of nearest relatives *wife Nadezhda Jakovl. Apt. 26, Furmanov Lane 5 Moscow*
17. Permanent and most recent place of residence *3d* [illegible] *Kalinin*

Right finger print

Work before Imprisonment

Institution or Enterprise	Position occupied	From	To
Drama theater Voronezh	*Lit. Consultant*	19	38
[illegible]			

I have been informed of the responsibility for the giving of false information

Signature of the prisoner *O.E. Mandel'shtam*

Заполняется администрацией

1. Кем осужден _Ос. АНКВД СССР_   2. Когда _2. 08 38_

3. За что и статья _КРД_   4. Срок _5_   с. _30 04_ 1938 г.

по. _30 04_ 1943

Начальник Урч _____   Исполнитель _____

Зачет рабочих дней по лагерям

кварт	19____ г. за время	дней	конец срока	расписка исполнит.
I	с____ по____			
II	с____ по____			
III	с____ по____			
IV	с____ по____			

кварт	19____ г. за время	дней	конец срока	расписка исполнит.
I	с____ по____			
II	с____ по____			
III	с____ по____			
IV	с____ по____			

кварт	19____ г. за время	дней	конец срока	расписка исполнит.
I	с____ по____			
II	с____ по____			
III	с____ по____			
IV	с____ по____			

кварт	19____ г. за время	дней	конец срока	расписка исполнит.
I	с____ по____			
II	с____ по____			
III	с____ по____			
IV	с____ по____			

кварт	19____ г. за время	дней	конец срока	расписка исполни
I	с____ по____			
II	с____ по____			
III	с____ по____			
IV	с____ по____			

кварт	19____ г. за время	дней	конец срока	расписка исполнит.
I	с____ по____			
II	с____ по____			
III	с____ по____			
IV	с____ по____			

*) к § 15

	Наименование	С какого времени и по какое	Ст От УК	В качестве кого работал
1 раз		с____ по____		
2 раз		с____ по____		
3 раз		с____ по____		

Регистратор

To be Filled Out by the Administration

1. By whom convicted *Special Board of the USSR NKVD*

2. When *August 2, 1938* 3. For what and which article *Counterrev.ary Activity*

4. Term *5* from *April 30* 193*8* through *April 30* 1934*3*

Head of the Administration of the Work Section _____ Responsible _____

Account of working days by camps

quarter	19 for time	days	end of period	signed by responsible
I	from _ through _			
II	from _ through _			
III	from _ through _			
IV	from _ through _			

quarter	19 for time	days	end of period	signed by responsible
I	from _ through _			
II	from _ through _			
III	from _ through _			
IV	from _ through _			

quarter	19 for time	days	end of period	signed by responsible
I	from _ through _			
II	from _ through _			
III	from _ through _			
IV	from _ through _			

quarter	19 for time	days	end of period	signed by responsible
I	from _ through _			
II	from _ through _			
III	from _ through _			
IV	from _ through _			

quarter	19 for time	days	end of period	signed by responsible
I	from _ through _			
II	from _ through _			
III	from _ through _			
IV	from _ through _			

quarter	19 for time	days	end of period	signed by respnsbl.
I	from _ through _			
II	from _ through _			
III	from _ through _			
IV	from _ through _			

*) to § 15

Desig-nation	From when to when	Arts. of Crm Cod	Worked as what
1st time	from to		
2nd time	from to		
3rd time	from to		

Registrar

FRONT

ВЫПИСКА ИЗ ПРОТОКОЛА

Особого совещания при Народном комиссаре внутренних дел СССР

от „ 2 "   августа   193 8 г.

СЛУШАЛИ	ПОСТАНОВИЛИ
77. Дело № 19390/ц о МАНДЕЛЬШТАМ Осипе Эмилье- виче, 1891 г.р. сын купца, б. эсер.	МАНДЕЛЬШТАМ Осипа Эмильевича- за к.-р. деятельность заключит в исправтрудлагерь сроком на ПЯТЬ лет, сч. срок с 30/IУ-38г. Дело сдать в архив.

Отв. секретарь Особого совещания

Т. им. Воровского. Н. 13015

BACK

Постановление особого
совещания читал О. Э. Мандельштам

Обыскан 8/8-38 г. Асеев

FRONT

EXCERPT FROM THE RECORD

of the Special Board attached to the People's Commissariat
of Internal Affairs of the USSR

of __August 2__ 193 _8_

HEARD	ORDERED
77. Case No. 19390/ts of Osip Emil'evich MANDEL'SHTAM born 1891, son of a merchant, former memer of the Social Revolutionary Party.	Osip Emil'evich MANDEL'SHTAM, for counter-revolutionary activity is to be confined in a corrective labor camp for a term of FIVE years, calculating the term from April 30, 1938. the file is to be deposited in the archive.

[SEAL]   **I. Shapiro**

Responsible Secretary of the Special Board

Vorovskii Press No. 13015

BACK

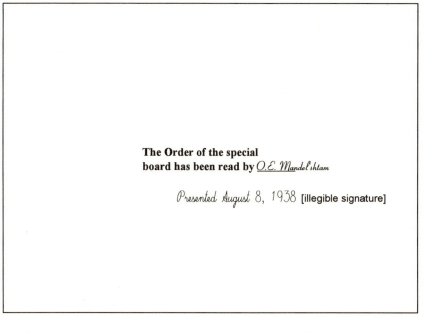

The Order of the special
board has been read by *O.E. Mandel'shtam*

Presented August 8, 1938 [illegible signature]

СССР

НАРОДНЫЙ КОМИССАРИАТ ВНУТРЕННИХ ДЕЛ
ГЛАВНОЕ УПРАВЛЕНИЕ ГОСУДАРСТВЕННОЙ БЕЗОПАСНОСТИ

Сфотографирован

Талон ордера №: 2817

30 Апрел дня 193*8* г.

Начальнику приема арестованных

Примите арестованного *Мандельштам*
Осипа Эмильевича

дело которого находится

справка: *64*

Зам. Народного Комиссара Внутренних Дел СССР

Начальник Второго Отдела ГУГБ

USSR

PEOPLE'S COMMISSARIAT
OF INTERNAL AFFAIRS
MAIN ADMINISTRATION OF STATE SECURITY

Photographed
Coupon of warrant No. 2817

30 April 1938

To the head of reception of arrestees

Receive the arrestee _____ *Mandel'shtam* _____

_____ *Osip Emil'evich* _____

whose file is located at

_____

Note: _64_ _____

[illegible signature]
Deputy People's Commissar of
Internal Affairs of the USSR

Head of the Second Department of the Main
Administration of State Security
[illegible signature]

65ъ5

ДЕСЯТЫЙ ОТДЕЛ ГУГБ НКВД СОЮЗА ССР

5/8   193 *8* г.   № *16023*

СЛУЖЕБНАЯ ЗАПИСКА

Начальнику _____ государственной безопасности
                                                                        тов. _____

Начальнику _____ тюрьмы ГУГБ
_____ государственной безопасности
                                                                        тов. _____

Арестованн ___ *Мандельштама О.Э.*

_____ авьте в _____ тюрьму ГУГБ.

_____ ите из

_____ оместите _____

_____ олировав от арестованн _____

Арестованн   числить за „   " отделением „   " отдела ГУГБ.

Начальник 10-го отдела ГУГБ НКВД

_____ государственной безопасности

М. П.

Начальник   отделения

_____ государственной безопасности

65 [illegible]

**TENTH DEPARTMENT OF THE MAIN ADMINISTRATION
OF THE USSR PEOPLE'S COMMISSARIAT OF INTERNAL AFFAIRS**

August 5   *193* 8   **No** *16023*

OFFICIAL RECORD

To the head   *of the Internal Prison*

Senior Lieutenant   of State Security

                Comrade   [illegible]

To the head   *of Butyrka*   Prison of the Main Administration of State Security

    Major   ~~of State Security~~

                Comrade   *Pustynskii*

Arrestee   ✓   *Mandel'shtam O E*

[Se]nd to   *Butyrka*   prison of the Main Administration of State Security

[Receiv]e from   *Internal prison*

[and p]lace   *in a general cell*

isolated from arrestee/s

                   4 / 4th /

Register the arrestee under the   division of the   department of the Main
Administration of State Security

**Head of the 10th Department of the Main Adminstration of State Security
Of the People's Commissariat of Internal Affairs**

Place
for
seal

   Major   [illegible signature]   of State Security

Head of the _____ division

                      of State Security

[faint triangular seal, with words "prison..," "USSR People's
Commissariat of Internal Affairs" and "No. 2."]

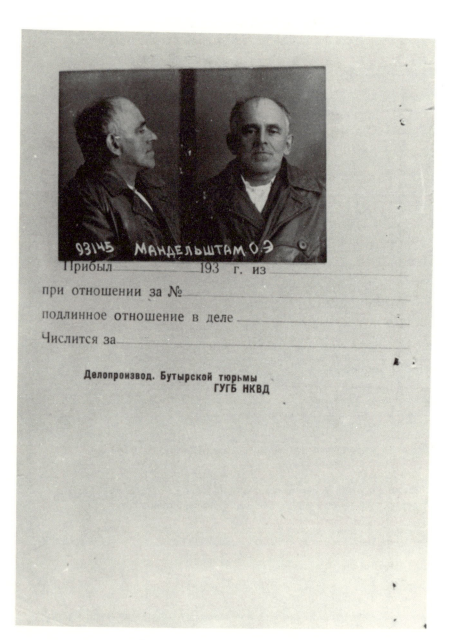

| [right profile photo] | [full face photo] |

93145 MANDEL'SHTAM O.E.

Arrived _____ 193   from _____

with transfer order No. _____

original transfer order in file _____

Registered under _____

Recordkeeping of Butyrka Prison
of the Main Adminstration of State Security of
the People's Commissariat of Internal Affairs

ПРОТОКОЛ ОТОЖДЕСТВЛЕНИЯ.-

193 г. Декабря м-ца 2... дня г. Владивосток.
Я старшим дактилоскоп ОУР РО УГБ НКВД по "ДАЛЬСТРОЙ" ОВ ФЕНЕВ
произвел сличение с отождествленными пальце-от счатками снятых на
дакто-карте умершего з/к 27 декабря 1938 г.
числящегося в ОК части ОЛП согласно ротной карточки по фамилии

Мандельштам Осип Эмильевич

с пальце-отпечат-
ками на дакто-карте, зарегистрированной на имя Мандельштам
Осипа Эмильевича
взятом из личного дела № 117799

ОКАЗАЛОСЬ: что строении по милярных линии, узоров и характерных особеннос-
тях пальце-от счатков по обоим снимаемым дакто-картам между собой
совершенного тождественна, означенных
фактдокумелтов 13 83495
17 73565   и принадлежит одно...
лицу и тому же лицу.

Ст дактилоскоп ОУР РО УГБ НКВД
по "ДАЛЬСТРОЙ":

RECORD OF IDENTITY.-

The _21st_ day of _December_ 193 CITY OF VLADIVOSTOK.

I, Senior Dactyloscopist of the Department of Administration of Labor of the Labor Division of the Administration of State Security of the Administration of the People's Commissariat of Internal Affairs for "Far [East] Construction]," [P]OVERENNOV, have performed a collation with identical fingerprints taken on the dactylocard of the deceased prisoner _____ _December 27, 1938_

registered in the health section of the department of camp clinics according to company card under the name _____
Mondel'shtam [sic] _Osip Emil'evich_
_____ with the fingerprints

on the dactylocard registered in the name _____ _Mondel'shtam_
_____ _Osip   Emil'evich_

from personal file No. _____ _117794_

IT APPEARS: that the structures on iliar lines, markings, and characteristic features of the fingerprints from both dactylocards are mutually _____
_____ _entirely identical. They are designated by fingerprint_
_____ _code 13/83445_ _____ and belong to __one_
_____ _/17 73565_
and the same person

SENIOR DACTYLOSCOPIST OF THE DEPARTMENT OF
ADMINISTRATION OF LABOR OF THE LABOR DIVISION
OF THE ADMINISTRATION OF STATE SECURITY OF THE
ADMINISTRATION OF THE PEOPLE'S COMMISSARIAT OF
INTERNAL AFFAIRS FOR "FAR [EAST] CONSTRUCTION":

Poverennov
/POVERENNOV/

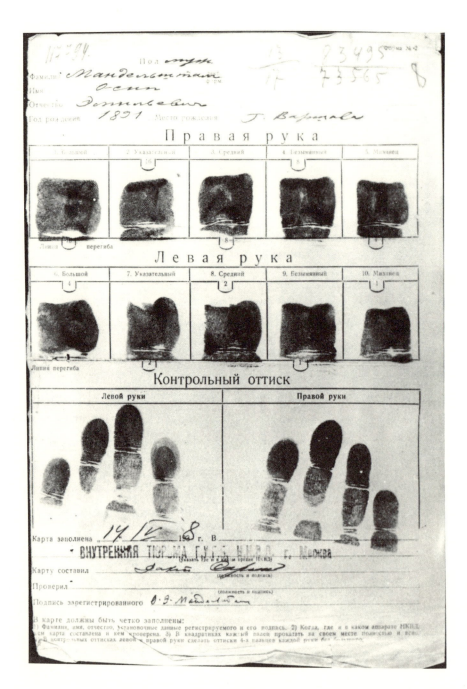

117794   13   83495   Form No. 2

     Sex _male_   17   73565

Last Name _Mandel'shtam_   dact.

First Name _Osip_   form.

Patrynymic _Emil'evich_

Year of birth _1891_   Place of birth _Warsaw_

Right Hand

1.Thumb	2. Index	3. Middle	4. Ring	5. Little
---|16|---		---|8|---		
---|16|--- Crease line		---|8|---		---|4|---

Left Hand

6.Thumb	7. Index	8. Middle	9. Ring	10.Little
---|4|---		---|2|---		---|1|---
---|2|--- Crease line		---|1|---		

Check Print

Left Hand	Right Hand

Card filled in _April 14_ 1938   At _____

INTERNAL PRISON OF THE MAIN ADMINISTRATION OF STATE SECUR-ITY OF THE PEOPLE'S COMMISSARIAT OF INTERNAL AFFAIRS MOSCOW

    (Indicate where and in which organ of the People's Commissariat of Internal Affairs)

Card prepared by _____ [illegible] [illegible]

                 (position and signature)

Verified by _____

                 (position and signature)

Signature of the registree _O.E. Mandel'shtam_

On the card the following should be filled in clearly:

1) Last name, first name, patronymic, indentifying data on the registree, and his signature. 2) When, where, and in what apparatus of the People's Commissariat of Internal Affairs and by whom the card was prepared and by whom verifed. 3) In the boxes, each finger should be rotated fully and clearly in its place. 4) In the check prints of the left and right hands take prints of the four fingers of each hand without the thumb.

FRONT

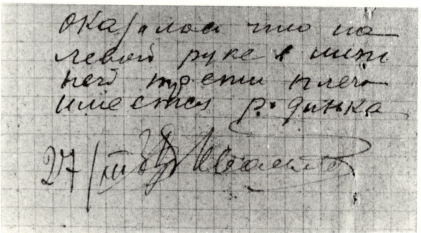

BACK

FRONT

Note

Prisoner Mendelshtam

was under treatment

since December 26 died

December 27 at 12:30

upon examination of the corpse

BACK

it appeared that on
the left arm on the lower
third of the upper arm
there is a birthmark

December 27, 1938 [illegible signature]

П О Л *М.*

Фамилия *Мандельштам*   д. форм

Имя   *Осип*

Отчество   *Эмильевич*

Место рождения *Умер 27/XII 38 г.*   Год рожд. *1891*

П р а в а я   р у к а

1. Большой	2 Указательный	3 Средний	4. Безымянный	5 Мизинец

Линия |16| перегиба |8| |4|

Л е в а я   р у к а

6. Большой	7 Указательный	8 Средний	9 Безымянный	10. Мизинец

Линия перегиба |2| |1|

Контрольный оттиск

Левой руки	Правой руки

Подпись зарегистрированного

Карта заполнена „*17*" *Декабря* 193*8* г.

В _*п/л Свитл НКВД Владивосток*_

(указать, где и в каком органе НКВД)

Карту составил _*Регист-ор*_

(должность и подписи)

Проверил

ПРИМЕЧАНИЕ: В верхней половине карты, на лицевой стороне в каждом квадратике должны быть прокатаны пальцы. В нижней половине—в квадратах под надписью „Контрольный оттиск" помещаются не прокатанные оттиски 4-х пальцев каждой руки без большого.

13   83495   F. No. 2

SEX *M.*   17   73565

Last Name *Mandel'shtam*   **D**. form { _____.

First Name *Osip*

Patrynymic *Emil'evich*

Place of birth *Died Dec. 27, '38*   Year of birth *1891*

Right Hand

1.Thumb	2. Index	3. Middle	4. Ring	5. Little
--------------	16	--------------	8	--------------------

------|16|-------------------------|8|-----------------------|4|------
Crease   **line**

Left Hand

6.Thumb	7. Index	8. Middle	9. Ring	10.Little
------	4	----------------------	2	--------------------------	1	----

--------------------|2|------------------------|1|--------
Crease   line

Check Print

Left Hand	Right Hand

Signature of the registree _____

Card filled in *December 27* 193**8**

At [illegible] *Northeast Corrective Labor Camps of the People's Commissariat of Internal Affairs Vladivostok*

(Indicate where and in which organ of the People's Commissariat of Internal Affairs)

Card prepared by *Registrar* [illegible] [illegible] _____
                              (position and signature)

Verified by _____

Note: In the upper half of the card, on the front, in each box, the fingers should be rotated. In the lower half—in the boxes under the title "Check Print" the nonrotated prints of the four fingers of each hand without the thumb are placed.

Прибыл этапом 12/Х-38   Помещен в стационар 25/XII-3...

А К Т № 1911

27/VII-38 г. Мы нижеподписавшиеся ВРАЧ НКВД-НСО Гор.мед ...льшеР....... составили настоящий акт о смерти
з/к умершего в больнице СП СБУТЛ НКВД.

1. Фамилия имя и отчество.   МСЦ ЛЯНШТАМ Осип Эмильевич

2. Год рождения   1891

3. Откуда происходит.   Польша.

4. Кем и когда осужден. С/С НКВД СССР 2/VIII-38 г.

5. Статья и срок.   КРД   5 .

6. Последнее место жительства.   г. Калинин

7. Причина смерти.   Паралич сердца е/к склероз
                      Труп вскрытию 27/XII-8 г.
виду болезни смерти труп вскрытию не подвергался

В Р А Ч ......

Зав мед больш.р....

Arrived from Moscow, Oct. 12, '38   Placed in infirmary Dec. 26, 1938

Certificate No. 1911

Dec. 27, '38. We the undersigned PHYSICIAN. KRESANOV Duty medic ·········
······duty officer·······prepared the present certificate on the death of
a prisoner who died in the hospital of the Department of Camp Polyclinics of
the Northeast Corrective Labor Camps of the People's Commissariat of
Internal Affairs.

1. Last name, first name, and patronymic.   MONDEL'SHTAM Osip Emil'evich
2. Year of birth   1891
3. Where from.   Poland
4. By whom and when convicted.   Special Board of the People's
   Commissariat of Internal Affairs of the USSR / August 2, 1938
5. Article and term.   Counter-revolutionary Activity 5 years.
6. Last place of residence.   Kalinin
7. Cause of death.   Stoppage of the heart arteriocerebrosclerosis
                Body fingerprinted Dec. 27, '38

In view of the obviousness of death the body was not subjected
to autopsy

        P H Y S I C I A N [illegible signature]
        DUTY MEDIC [illegible signature]

                            Dec. 27 /27

FRONT

> В главное Управление лагерей.
>
> Мне известно, что мой муж заключенный Мандельштам Осип Эмильевич умер во Владивостоке (С.В.И.Т.Л. 11 барак. 5 лет КРД.), т.к. мне был возвращен денежный перевод „за смертью адресата". Дата смерти определяется между 15/XII 38г и 10/I 1939г.
>
> Прошу управление лагерей проверить мои сведенья и выдать мне оффициальную справку о смерти О.Э. Мандельштама.
>
>   Надежда Мандельштам.
>
> Ответ прошу сообщить по адресу:
> Москва Старосадский № 10 кв 3
>   Александру Эмильевичу Мандельштам
>
> У меня в данное время адреса нет, т.к. временная моя прописка в Москве кончилась и я ищу помещение под Москвой.

BACK

North East Corrective Labor Camps

3/2899 First Dept.

Acc'ting Assignment Div.

Feb. 7, 1939

To the Main Administration of Camps

| Inspect. |
| [illegible] NKVD GULAG |
| Feb. 9, 1939 |

V3/2844

I know that my husband, Mandel'shtam, Osip Emilevich, died in Vladivostok (North East Corrective Labor Camps, 11th Barracks 5 years for Counter-revolutionary activity), since a money transfer was returned to me "because of the death of the addressee." The date of death must be between December 15, 1938 and January 10, 1939.

I request that the administration of camps verify my information and issue me an official certificate on the death of O.E. Mandel'shtam.

Nadezhda Mandel'shtam

I request that the answer be communicated to the address:
Alexander Emil'evich Mandel'shtam
Starosadskii No. 10, Apt. 3, Moscow

At the present time I do not have an address, since my temporary residence permit in Moscow has expired and I am seeking lodging near Moscow.

Administration . . . . . . of Internal Affairs	
Date	Entry Number

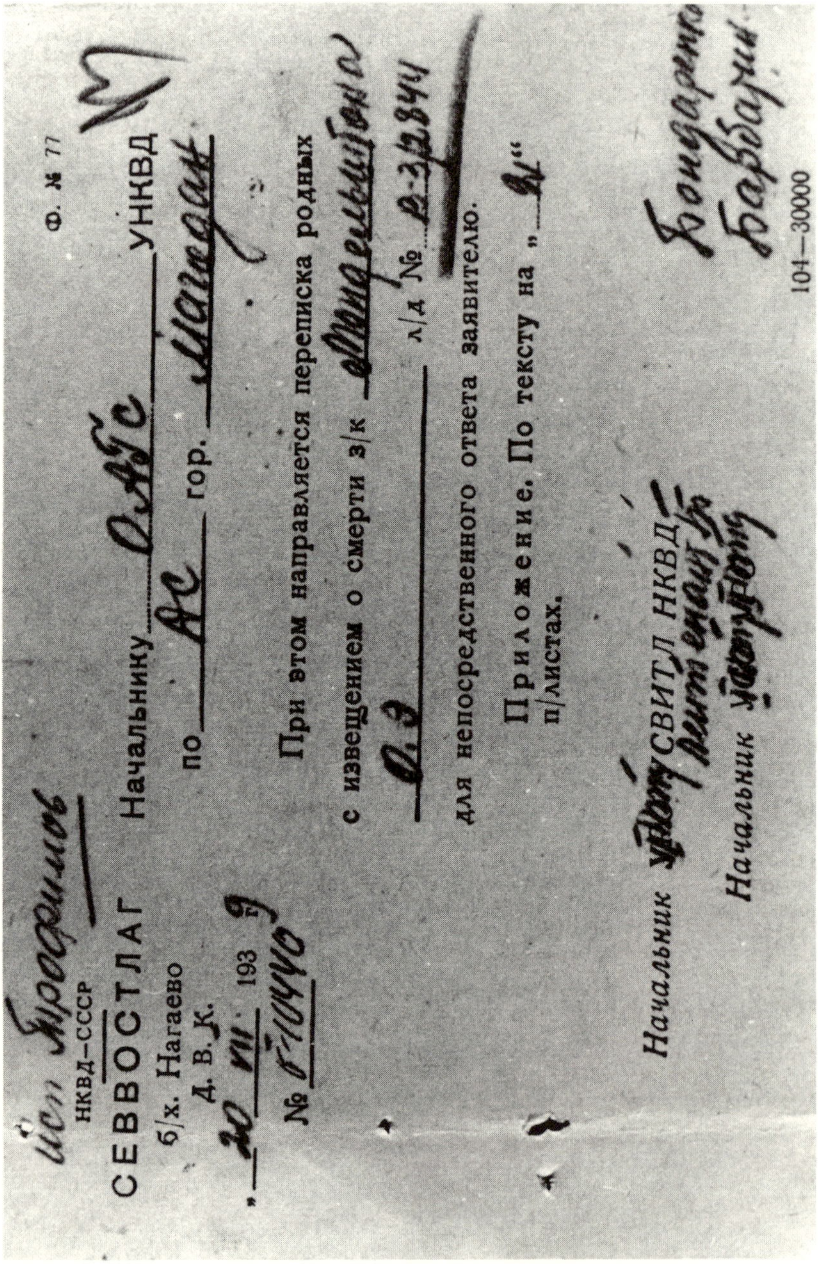

Ф. № 77

НКВД–СССР

СЕВВОСТЛАГ

б/х. Нагаево

Д. В. К.

"20" VII 1939 г.

№

Начальнику ____ УНКВД

по ____ гор. ____

При этом направляется переписка родных

с извещением о смерти з/к ____

____ л/д № ____

для непосредственного ответа заявителю.

Приложение. По тексту на "____"

п/листах.

Начальник УРО СВИТЛ НКВД

Начальник

104—30000

Form No. 77

by Trofimov

People's Commissariat of Internal Affairs -- USSR

NORTH EAST CAMPS

b/kh. Nagaevo
Far East Province

July 20 1939
No. 5-10440

To the Head of the Department of Civil Status Registration **of the Administration of the People's Commissariat of Internal Affairs for** the Far North city of Magadan

Attached is the correspondence of relatives with notification of the death of prisoner Mandel'shtam O.E. file No. 9-3/2844 for a direct answer to the applicant.

1st Dep't

Attachment. Text on 2 pages.

Head of the Accounting-Assignment Department of the Northeast Corrective Labor Camps of the People's Commissariat of Internal Affairs

Lieutenant [illegible]   Bondarenko

Head of the Administration of the Statistical Department of the Accounting Assignment Department 1st Dept., 2nd Div.   Barbarin

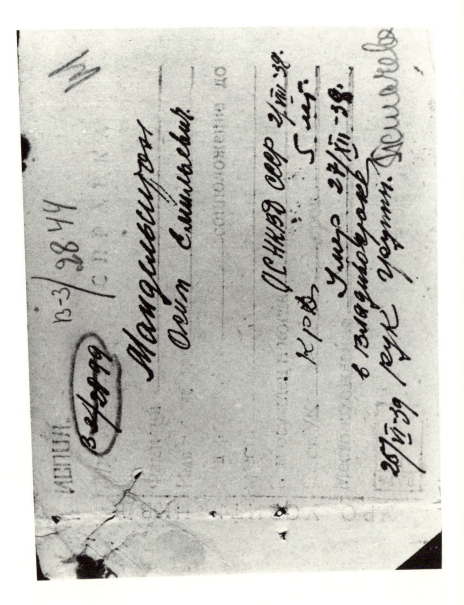

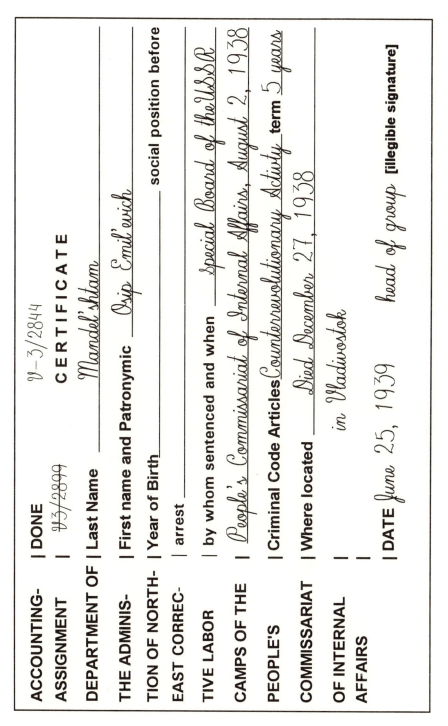

ACCOUNTING- | DONE

ASSIGNMENT | У-3/2899

Ⴧ-3/2844

DEPARTMENT OF | Last Name   *Mandel'shtam*

C E R T I F I C A T E

THE ADMINIS- | First name and Patronymic   *Osip Emil'evich*

TION OF NORTH- | Year of Birth _____ social position before

EAST CORREC- | arrest _____

TIVE LABOR | by whom sentenced and when   *Special Board of the USSR*

CAMPS OF THE | *People's Commissariat of Internal Affairs, August 2, 1938*

PEOPLE'S | Criminal Code Articles *Counterrevolutionary Activity* **term** *5 years*

COMMISSARIAT | Where located   *Died December 27, 1938*

| *in Vladivostok*

OF INTERNAL |

AFFAIRS |

| DATE *June 25, 1939*   head of group [illegible signature]

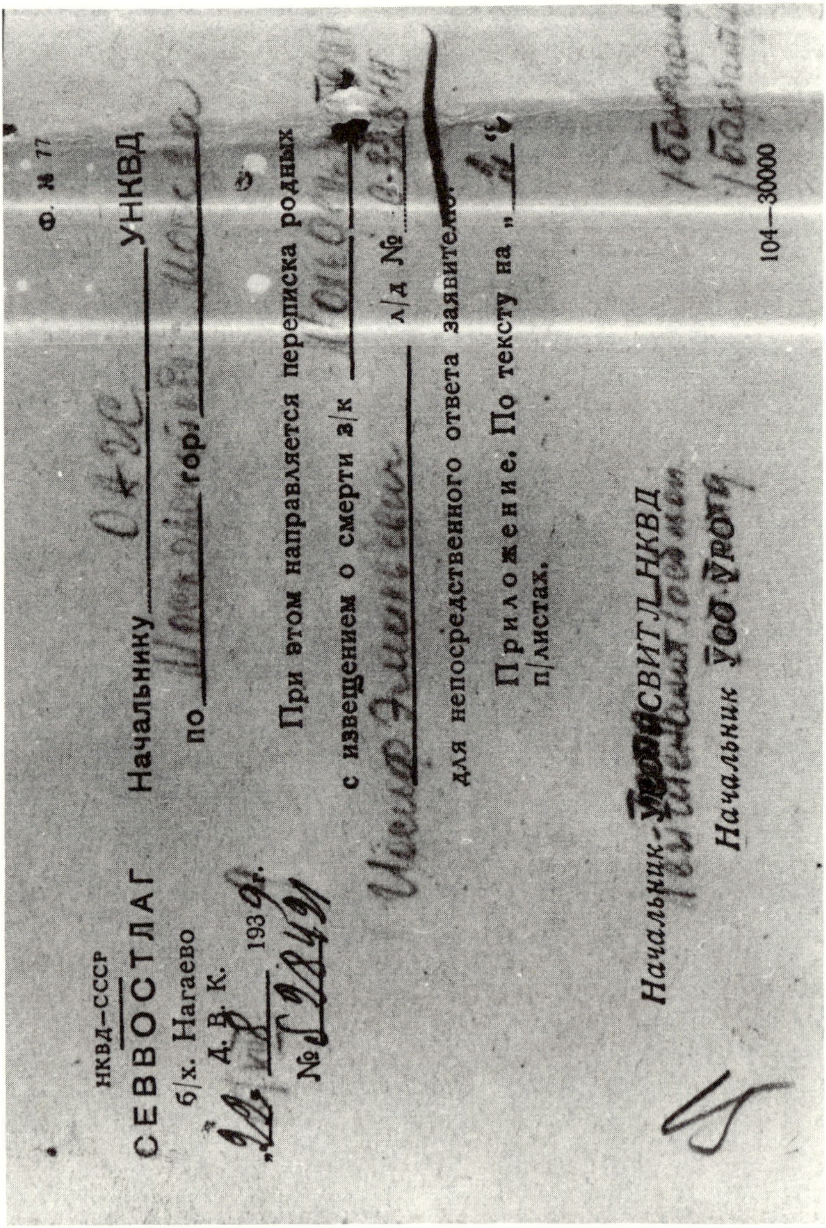
НКВД—СССР
СЕВВОСТЛАГ
б/х. Нагаево
Д. В. К.
„12" ______ 1939 г.
№ ______

Ф. № 77

Начальнику ______ УНКВД

по ______ гор.

При этом направляется переписка родных

с извещением о смерти з/к ______

______ л/д № ______

для непосредственного ответа заявителю.

Приложение. По тексту на „ ______ " п/листах.

Начальник-УРО СВИТЛ НКВД

Начальник УОО УРО

104—30000

Form No. 77

People's Commissariat of Internal Affairs – USSR

NORTH EAST CAMPS

b/kh. Nagaevo

Far East Province

August 22 1939

No. 52/8421

To the Head _of the Department of Civil Status Registration_

of the Administration of the **People's Commissariat**

of Internal Affairs for _the Moscow Region_

city of _Moscow_

Attached is correspondence of relatives

with notification of the death of prisoner _Mendel'shtam_

Iosif Emil'evich   file No. _V-3-2844_

for a direct answer to the applicant.

Attachment.   Text on _2_

pages.

Head of the Accounting-Assignment Department   _1st Dep't_

of the Administration of Northeast Corrective   _Lieutenant[illegible]_   _Bondarenko_

Labor Camps of the People's Commissariat

of Internal Affairs

Head of the Administration of Statistics   _1st Dep't 2nd Dep't_   _Barbarin_

104-30000

Московский б.3

форма № 1.

Управление Сев. Восточных Исправительно-Трудовых лагерей Н. К. В. Д.

Учетно-статистическая карточка

Личное дело № *117794*

Прибыл в лагерь *12. X* 193*8* г.

Место для фотокарточки

Категория содержания				
Категория трудоспособ.	*СФТ*			

ОСОБЫЕ ПРИМЕТЫ

1. Фамилия и кличка *Мандельштам*
2. Имя и отчество *Осип Эмильевич*
3. Год рожд. *1891* Место рождения и приписки *Польша*

1. Рост *средний*
2. Телослож. *полн.*
3. Цвет волос *седые*
4. Цвет глаз *карие*
5. Нос *с горбинкой*
6. Прочие приметы

4. Образование { Общее *высшее*
   Специальное
5. Гражданство *СССР* Национальность *еврей*
6. Специальность { Общая *писатель*
   Узкая *поэт*
   Отж *9л*
7. Постанов. квалфикац. комиссии:

8. Какие языки знает кроме родного *рус., франц. нем.*
9. Социальное происхождение *сын купца*
10. Социальное положение *писатель*
11. Партийность

12. Служба в армиях { Старой
   Белой
   Красной
13. Служба в судебн. орган. и НКВД
14. Время ареста *2-V-38*
15. Прежняя судимость *судился* который раз в лагере*)
16. Семейное положение *женат* Указать фамилии и адреса ближних родственников *Ж. Надежда Яковлевна г. Москва труб*
17. Постоянное и последнее место жительства:

Работа до заключения

Учреждение или предприятие	Занимаемая должность	От	До
Драм театр г. Воронеже по дечане	*лит. консул.*	*1938*	*Арест*

Об ответственности за дачу ложных сведений мне объявлено

Подпись заключенного *О. Э. Мандельштам*

Moscow car 3

form No. 1

Administration of the North East Corrective Labor Camps of the People's Commissariat of Internal Affairs
Statistical Record Card
Personal File No. _17794_.

arrived at the camp _October 12_ 1938

Category of maintenance				
Category of	*mod.*			
Ability to work	*phys.lab.*			

Place for Photo

1. Last name and nickname *Mandel'shtam*

2. First name and patronymic *Osip Emil'evich*

3. Year of birth _1891_ Place of birth and registation _Poland_

4. Education   (General _____ *Higher* _____
    (Specialized _____

5. Citizenship _USSR_____ Nationality _Jew_

6. Specialty   (General _____ *writer and*
    (Narrow _____ *poet*
    (Experience _29 years_

7. Ruling of the skill evaluation commission: _____

8. What foreign languages do you know other than your native language? _Russian, French, German, Italian, Spanish_

9. Social origin _son of a merchant_

10. Social position _writer_

11. Party membership _none_

12. Service in armies   {Old -
    {White _____
    {Red -

13. Service in judicial bodies and NKVD _____

14. Time of detention _May 2, 1938_

15. Previous convictions _under Art. 58_ number of times in camp *)____

16. Family position _married_ indicate names and addresses of close relatives _wife Nadezhda Iakovlevna   Apt. 26, 5 Furmanov lane, Moscow_

17. Permanent and latest residence _3t [illegible] Kalinin_

DISTINCTIVE FEATURES

|1. Height _medium_
|2. Build _normal_
|3. Hair _grey_
|4. Eyes _hazel_
|5. Nose _aquiline_
|6. Other _back_ _and abdomen covered_ _with hair_ _baldness on_ _head_

Right Thumb print

Work Before Imprisonment

Institution or Enterprise	Position occupied	From	To
Drama theater Voronezh	Literary consultant	1938	Arrest
[illegible]			

I have been informed of the responsibility for giving false information
signature of the prisoner _O.E. Mandel'shtam_

K-0 COVER

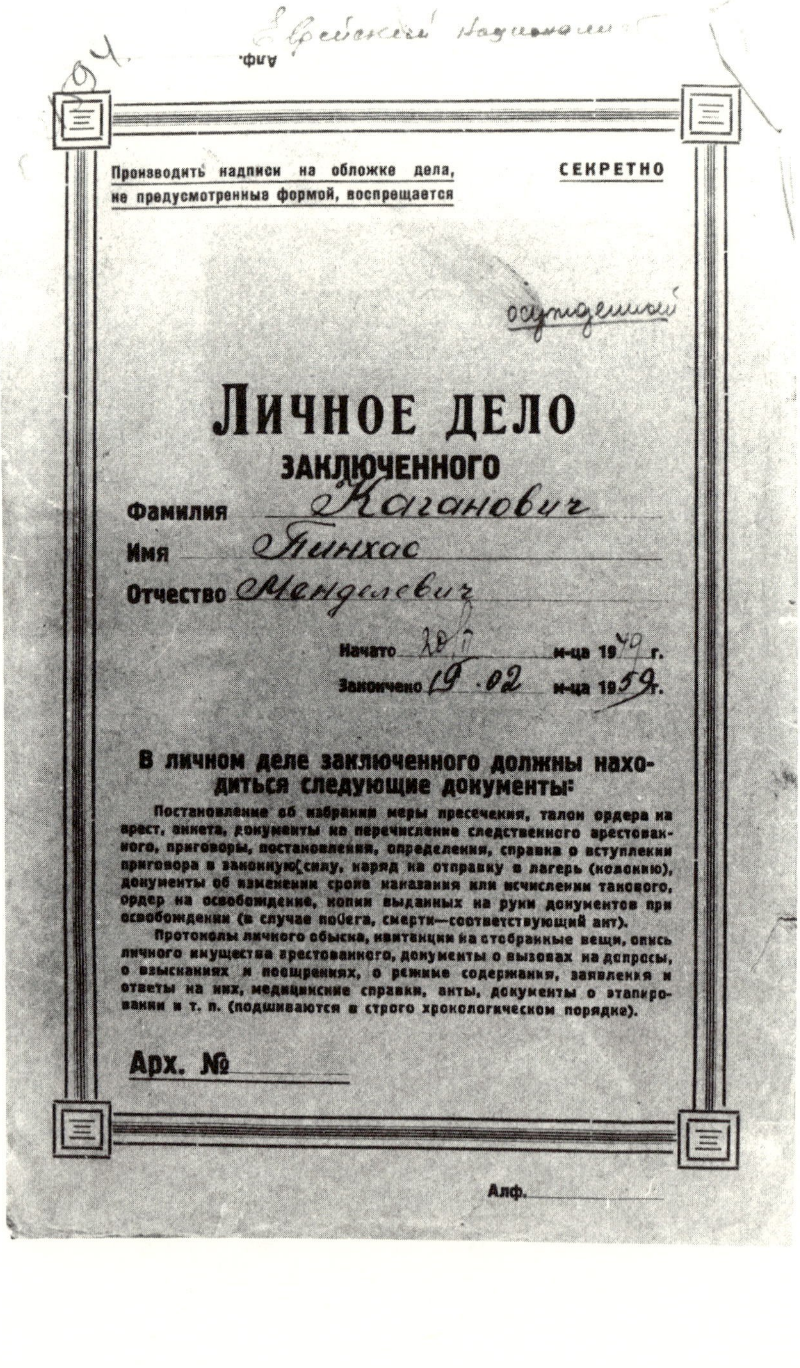

Еврейский националист

Производить надписи на обложке дела, не предусмотренные формой, воспрещается

СЕКРЕТНО

осужденный

ЛИЧНОЕ ДЕЛО

ЗАКЛЮЧЕННОГО

Фамилия Каганович

Имя Пинхас

Отчество Менделевич

Начато 20.II **м-ца** 1949 **г.**

Закончено 19.02 **м-ца** 1959 **г.**

В личном деле заключенного должны находиться следующие документы:

Постановление об избрании меры пресечения, талон ордера на арест, анкета, документы на перечисление следственного арестованного, приговоры, постановления, определения, справка о вступлении приговора в законную силу, наряд на отправку в лагерь (колонию), документы об изменении срока наказания или исчислении такового, ордер на освобождение, копии выданных на руки документов при освобождении (в случае побега, смерти—соответствующий акт).

Протоколы личного обыска, квитанции на отобранные вещи, опись личного имущества арестованного, документы о вызовах на допросы, о взысканиях и поощрениях, о режиме содержания, заявления и ответы на них, медицинские справки, акты, документы о этапировании и т. п. (подшиваются в строго хронологическом порядке).

Арх. №

Алф.

021594

Jewish Nationality

SECRET

convicted

Personal File
of the prisoner

Last name _____ *Kaganovich* _____
First name _____ *Pinkhas* _____
Patronymic _____ *Mendelevich* _____

Begun _*Feb. 20*_ 19 *49*
Finished _*Feb. 19*_ 19*59*

The following documents must be in
the personal file of a prisoner

Order on selection of a measure of restraint, coupon of the warrant for arrest, questionnaire, documents for the transfer of an investigation detainee, sentences, orders, decisions, note on the entry of a sentence into legal force, order for transfer to a camp (or colony), documents on changing the period of punishment or its calculation, order for release, copies of documents handed over upon release (in case of escape or death--the corresponding official statement).

The records of personal search, receipts for items taken, a list of personal property of the detainee, documents on summonses for questioning, on penalties and rewards, on the type of custody, requests and answers to them, medical notes, official statements, documents on transport, etc. (sewn in strictly chronological order).

Archive No. _____

Арестованному не объявлять

Секретно

ИЗВЕЩЕНИЕ № _2191_   _1_

Начальнику _Лефор_ тюрьмы _мгб_

тов. _Иокову_

Арестованного _Каганович_
(фамилия, имя,

Пинхае Менделевича
отчество)

год рождения _1884_ , дело

которого направлено на рассмотрение

в _особ. Совещ. при мгб_
ссср.

после осуждения к лишению свободы надле-

жит отправить в **ОСОБЫЙ** лагерь (**ОСОБУЮ**

тюрьму).

Начальника _отдел „б" мгб ссср_
(Отдела „А" МГБ–УМГБ, Управления Отдела

полковник _Титов_
Контрразведки МГБ, Охраны МГБ жел.-дор.-водного бассейна)

Ар „_____" _____ 194 г.

Извещение подшивается к личному делу

заключенного первым листом.

NOTICE No. _2191_

To the Head of _Lefortovo_ **prison** _of the MGB_

Comrade _Ionov_

Arrestee _Kaganovich_

(last name, first name,

Pinkhas Mendeleevich

patronymic)

year of birth _1884._ , whose case has been sent for

consideration

to _the Special Board attached to the Ministry_

of State Security of the USSR

after sentencing to deprivation of freedom is to be sent to
a SPECIAL camp (or SPECIAL prison).

| Entry No. _2971_ |
| _Oct. 6_ **194**_9_ |
| Lefortovo Prison |
| USSR NKVD |

Head _of Department "A" of the USSR MGB_

(Dep't "A" of the MGB—Administration of the MGB, Administration-Dep't)

colonel **Titov** _Titov_

of Counterintelligence of the MGB, of MGB Railway-Water-Basin Guard)

_____ 194

This notice is to be sewn to the personal file of the prisoner as the first page.

К сведению начальника тюрьмы.

1. Извещение является предупреждением о том, что указанного в извещении арестованного, после осуждения к лишению свободы, надлежит направить в **особый лагерь или особую тюрьму.**

2. **Отправка** осужденных в особый лагерь или особую тюрьму **производится** по **вступлении приговора в законную силу, по персональным нарядам ГУЛАГа или Тюремного Управления МВД СССР.**

3. **Для получения наряда** на отправку нужно от извещения **оторвать талон,** заполнить его и направить в Отдел „А" МГБ—УМГБ или учетный аппарат другого органа МГБ, который вел следствие по делу.

4. На осужденных Особым совещанием наряды поступают в тюрьму вместе с выписками из решений Особого совещания.

For the Information of the
Head of the Prison.

1. This notice is a warning that the arrestee indicated in the notice, after sentencing to deprivation of freedom, is to be sent to **a special camp or special prison**.

2. **Dispatch** of convicts to a special camp or special prison **shall be done** upon **the entry of the sentence into legal force** under **individual orders of the GULAG [the Main Administration of Camps] or of the Prison Administration of the Ministry of Internal Affairs of the USSR.**

3. **To receive an order** for dispatch it is necessary **to tear off the coupon** from the notice, fill it out, and send it to Department A of the Ministry of State Security--Administration of the Ministry of State Security or to the record-keeping staff of the other organ of the Ministry of State Security that conducted the investigation of the case.

4. For persons convicted by the Special Board, the orders arrive at the prison together with the extracts from the decisions of the Special Board.

СССР

рство ГОСУДАРСТВЕННОЙ БЕЗОПАСНОСТИ

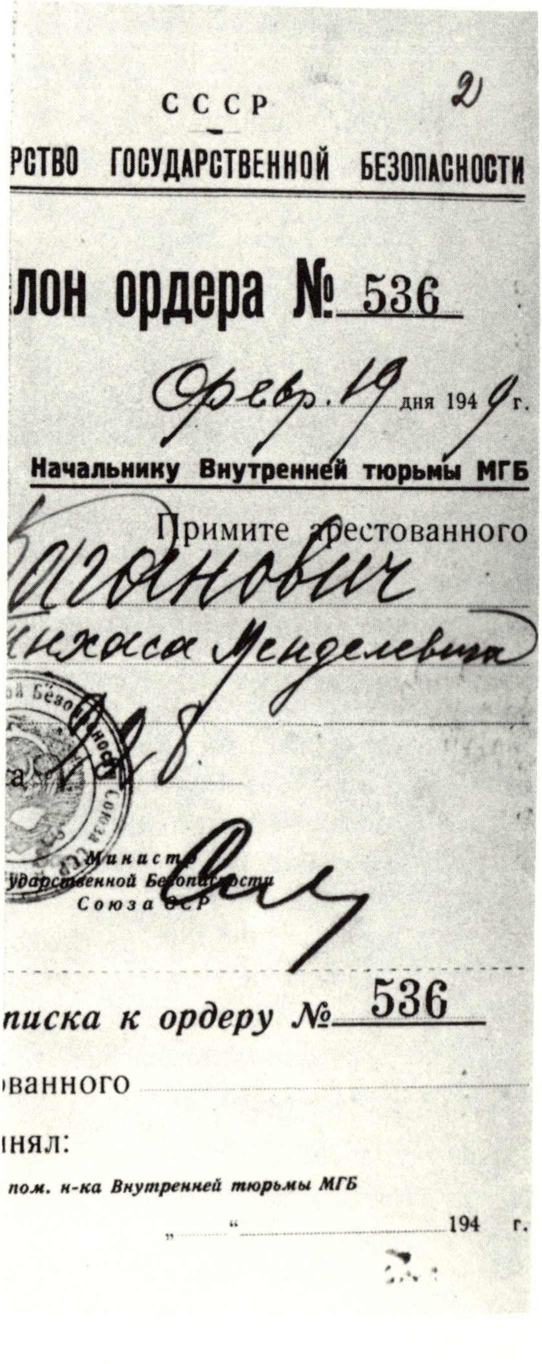

лон ордера № 536

Февр. 19 дня 194 9 г.

Начальнику Внутренней тюрьмы МГБ

Примите арестованного

[handwritten signatures]

Министр
ударственной Безопасности
Союза ССР

писка к ордеру № 536

ованного

нял:

пом. н-ка Внутренней тюрьмы МГБ

" "   194 г.

USSR

MINISTRY OF STATE SECURITY

===================================

Coupon of warrant No. 536

Feb. 19 194_9_

**To the HEAD of the Internal Prison of
Ministry of State Security**

Receive the arrestee

Kaganovich

Pinkhas Mendelevich

Note _228_

**Minister
of State Security
of the USSR**

- -

Extract for order No. _536_

Arrestee _____

[Receiv?]ed:

. . . _Assistant Head of the Internal Prison of the
Ministry of State Security_

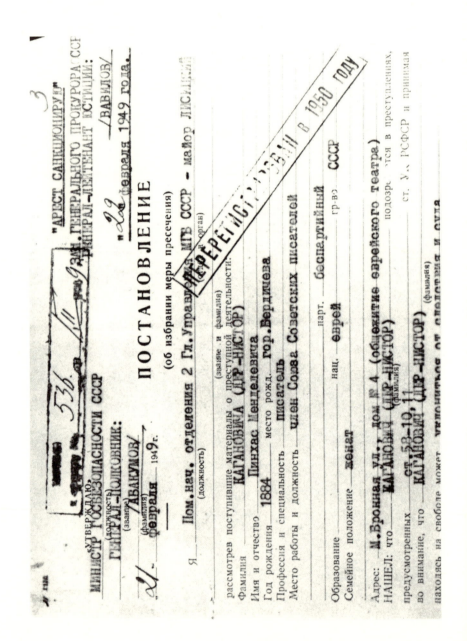

"АРЕСТ САНКЦИОНИРУЮ"

Зам.Генерального Прокурора СССР

Генерал-лейтенант юстиции:

/ВАВИЛОВ/

"___ февраля 1949 года.

УТВЕРЖДАЮ;

МИНИСТР Госбезопасности СССР

ГЕНЕРАЛ-ПОЛКОВНИК:

(должность)

/АБАКУМОВ/

(звание)   (фамилия)

"___ февраля 1949г.

ПОСТАНОВЛЕНИЕ

(об избрании меры пресечения)

ПЕРЕРЕГИСТРИРОВАН в 1950 году

Я ___ Пом.нач. отделения 2 Гл.Управления МГБ СССР – майор ЛИСИЦКИЙ

(должность)   (звание и фамилия)

рассмотрев поступившие материалы о преступной деятельности:

Фамилия ___ КАГАНОВИЧА (ШР-ИСТОР)

Имя и отчество ___ Пинхас Менделевича

Год рождения ___ 1884 ___ место рожд. ___ гор.Бердичева.

Профессия и специальность ___ писатель

Место работы и должность ___ член Союза Советских писателей

парт. ___ беспартийный ___ гр-во ___ СССР

Образование ___ нац. ___ еврей

Семейное положение ___ женат

Адрес: ___ М.Бронная ул., дом № 4 (общежитие еврейского театра)

НАШЕЛ: что ___ КАГАНОВИЧ (ШР-ИСТОР) ___ подозре...тся в преступлениях,
(фамилия)

предусмотренных ___ ст.58-10,11 ___ ст. У.. РСФСР и принима...
(фамилия)

во внимание, что ___ КАГАНОВИЧ (ШР-ИСТОР)
(фамилия)

находясь на свободе может уклониться от следствия и суда

"I APPROVE"

MINISTER OF STATE SECURITY OF THE USSR
(position)
COLONEL-GENERAL:
(rank)
/AVAKUMOV/
(last name)
February 21 194 9

"DETENTION APPROVED"

DEPUTY PROCURATOR GENERAL OF THE USSR
LIEUTENANT GENERAL OF JUSTICE:
/VAVILOV/
February 22 1949

ORDER

(on the selection of a measure of restraint)

I, Deputy Head of the 2nd Main Administration of the USSR Ministry of State Security—
(position)

Major Lisitskii
(rank and name)

having considered material received concerning criminal activity of:

Last name   KAGANOVICH (DER-NISTOR)

First name and patronymic   Pinkhas Mendelevich

Year of birth   1884   place of birth   Berdichev

Occupation and specialty   writer

Place of work and position   member of the Union of Soviet Writers

Education _____ nationality ___ Jew ___ party ___ none

Family position   married   citizenship   USSR

Address: Malaia Bronnaia St.,No. 4 (dormitory of the Jewish Theater)

HAVE FOUND: that   KAGANOVICH (DER-NISTOR)   is suspected of the crimes
(last name)

defined by   Art. 58-10,11   Articles of the RSFSR Criminal Code and taking

into account that   KAGANOVICH (DER-NISTOR)

being at liberty might   avoid investigation and trial

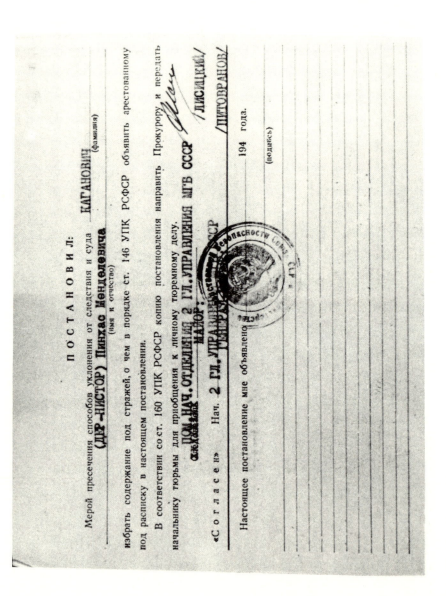

ПОСТАНОВИЛ:

Мерой пресечения способов уклонения от следствия и суда   КАГАНОВИЧ
(фамилия)

(ДЯР -НИСТОР) Пинхас Менделевича
(имя и отчество)

избрать содержание под стражей, о чем в порядке ст. 146 УПК РСФСР объявить арестованному

под расписку в настоящем постановлении.

В соответствии со ст. 160 УПК РСФСР копию постановления направить Прокурору и передать

начальнику тюрьмы для приобщения к личному тюремному делу.

ПОМ.НАЧ.ОТДЕЛЕНИЯ 2 ГЛ.УПРАВЛЕНИЯ МГБ СССР

МАЙОР: /ЛИСИЦКИЙ/

«Согласен»   Нач. 2 ГЛ.УПРАВЛЕНИ... ...СР

ГЕНЕРАЛ-...   /ПИТОВРАНОВ/

Настоящее постановление мне объявлено   194   года.

(подпись)

HAVE ORDERED:

As a measure of restraint from means of avoiding investigation and trial

(DER-NISTOR)   Pinkhas Mendelevich _____   by KAGANOVICH _____
                                                                    (last name)
(first name and patronymic)

to select detention under guard, about which, according to the procedure of Art. 146 of the RSFSR Criminal Procedure Code the person detained is to be notified against his signature on the present order..

In accordance with Art. 160 of the RSFSR Criminal Procedure Code a copy of this order is to be sent to the Procurator and given to the head of the prison for attachment to the personal prison file.

ASS''T HEAD OF DEPARTMENT OF THE 2nd MAIN ADMINISTRATION

OF THE USSR MINISTRY OF STATE SECURITY   *Lisitskii*   /LISITSKII/

InxveXXXgaXoX _____   MAJOR:

"A g r e e d"   Head OF THE 2ND MAIN ADMINISTRATION OF THE USSR MVD   /PITOVRANOV/

MAJOR-GENERAL

[MGB SEAL]

This order was presented to me on _____ 194____

_____
(signature)

Орг.. НКГБ

Приб 19/п 49. 6 20 25.

Передавать анкету для заполнения арестованному — запрещается. Заполняется со
слов арестованного и проверяется по до-
кументам.

Ч

Анкета арестованного

1. Фамилия, имя и от-
чество.

Когонович
Пинхас Менделевич

2. Год и место рож-
дения.

1884 года рождения г. Бердичев
Житомирская обл

3. Постоянное место
жительства до аре-
ста (подробный ад-
рес).

Москва
село, город, улица, дом №, кварт. №
район *Малая Бронная дом 4.*
область, край

4. Профессия и спе-
циальность.

Писатель

5. Последнее место ра-
боты или род заня-
тий до ареста. Если
не работал, когда
и откуда уволен.

Работал на дому

6. Национальность.

еврей

7. Гражданство (при
отсутствии паспорта
указать, какой доку-
мент удостоверяет
гражданство или за-
писано со слов).

а) гражд. (подд.). *СССР*

б) паспорт серии   №

выдан

8. Партийность.

б/п.   с . . . . . года

9. Образование общее
и специальное (подчерк-
нуть) и указать что
закончил.

высшее, среднее, низшее *Домашнее*
специальное

10. Социальное и поли-
тическое прошлое.

из купцов

11. Судимость (состоял
под судом и след-
ствием, где, когда,
за что, приговор).

Со слов не судим

Arrived Feb. 19, '49 at 20:25

Organ of the NKGB _____
_____
_____

Handing this form to the arrestee to fillout is forbidden. The form is to be filled out from the statements of the arrestee and checked against documents.

Arrestee Form

1. Last name, first name, and patronymic	*Kaganovich* *Pinkhas Mendelevich*
2. Year and place of birth	*born 1884 in Berdichev* *Zhitomir Region*
3. Permanent place of residence before arrest (full address)	*Moscow* village, city, street, house no., apt. no. district *Malaia Bronnaia 4* region, province
4. Occupation and specialty	*Writer*
5. Last place of work or type of occupation before arrest. If not working when and from where discharged	*Worked at home*
6. Nationality	*Jew*
7. Citizenship (if no passport, indicate what document confirms citizenship or if based on statement)	a) citizenship (subject of) *USSR* b) passport series No. issued
8. Party membership	*none* since the year
9. Education, general and specialized (underline) and indicate what he completed.	higher, secondary, primary *Home* specialized
10. Social and political past	*from the merchants*
11. Criminal record (tried, investigated, where, when, for what, sentence)	*States that he has no criminal record*

12. Участие в отечественной войне (где, когда, в качестве кого).	Нет
13. Был ли на оккупированной территории противником (указать: где, когда, что делал).	Нет

14. СОСТАВ СЕМЬИ

Степень родства	Фамилия, имя, отчество, год и место рождения	Место жительства, работы и должность
Отец	Умер	
Мать	Умерла	
Жена (муж)	Сиголовская Елене Клементьевна 1905	Москва Малая Проннал дом Ч.
Сын Дети	Каганович Иосиф Пейхасович 1923	Чучонка гор Певек
Братья, сестры	Каганович хана Менделеевна 1890.	г. Киев ул. Воровского 16.

12. Participation in the fatherland war (where, when, and as what).	No
13. Was he on territory occupied by the enemy (indicate: where, when, and what he did).	No

14. Family

Relation	Last name, first name, patronymic, year and place of birth	Place of residence of work & job
Father	Died	
Mother	Died	
Wife (husband)	Sigolovskaia, Elena Klement'evna 1905	Moscow Malaia Bronnaia 4
Son Children	Kaganovich, Iosif Penkhasovich 1923	Chukhotka, City of Pevek
Brothers, sisters	Kaganovich, Khana Mendeleevna 1890	Kiev, 16 Vorovskii St.

15. СЛОВЕСНЫЙ ПОРТРЕТ (нужное подчеркнуть)

1. **Рост:** высокий (171—180 см), очень высокий (свыше 180 см), низкий (155—164 см), очень низкий (до 154 см), средний (165—170 см).

2. **Фигура:** толстая, полная, средняя, худощавая, тонкая.

3. **Плечи:** приподнятые, опущенные, горизонтальные.

4. **Шея:** короткая, длинная, заметен зоб, выступает кадык.

5. **Цвет волос:** белокурые, светлорусые, русые, темнорусые, черные, рыжие, с проседью, седые.

6. **Цвет глаз:** голубые, серые, зеленоватые, светлокарие, карие, черные.

7. **Лицо:** круглое, овальное, прямоугольное, треугольное, пирамидальное, ромбовидное.

8. **Лоб:** высокий, низкий, прямой, скошенный, выступающий.

9. **Брови:** прямые, дугообразные, извилистые — широкие, узкие, сросшиеся.

10. **Нос:** малый, большой — толстый, тонкий, широкий. Спинка носа: вогнутая, прямая, выпуклая с горбинкой. Основание носа: приподнятое, горизонтальное, опущенное.

11. **Рот:** малый, большой. Углы рта: опущены, приподняты.

12. **Губы:** тонкие, толстые, отвисание нижней губы, приподнятость верхней.

13. **Подбородок:** скошенный, прямой, выступающий, раздвоенный, с ямкой, с поперечной бороздой.

14. **Уши:** малые, большие — овальные, треугольные, квадратные, круглые. Оттопыренность ушей: верхняя, нижняя, общая. Мочка уха: сросшаяся, отдельная, наклонная, угловатая, овальная.

16. Особые приметы *Шрам на среднем пальце правой руки на первом суставе*

физические недостатки: увечья, повреждения:

приметы: наросты, бородавки, лишние пальцы, пятна, рубцы, шрамы, болезненные

движения тела, плешивость, ассиметрия лица, разноцветность глаз и другие

татуировки (описание)

17. Прочие особенности и привычки *Незамечено*

картавит, заикается, грызет ногти,

различные пальцевые манипуляции, жестикулирует (указать как), автоматизм,

харкает, сплевывает и т. д. и т. п.

18. Когда арестован *19-февраля* 194 *9* г. ордер № *536*

19. Основание ареста

указать наименование документа, орган и дату

20. За кем зачислен *2/ч по ОВД МГБ СССР.*

15. **PORTRAIT IN WORDS** (underline)

1. **Height:** tall (171-180 cm.), very tall (over 180 cm.), short (155-164 cm.), very short (up to 154 cm.), average (165-170 cm.).

2. **Figure:** fat, full, average, slim, thin.

3. **Shoulders:** raised, lowered, horizontal.

4. **Neck:** short, long, noticeable goiter, protruding Adam's apple.

5. **Hair color:** blond, light brown, brown, dark brown, black, red, greying, grey.

6. **Eye color:** blue, grey, greenish, light hazel, hazel, dark.

7. **Face:** round, oval, square, triangular, pyramidal, rhomboid.

8. **Forehead:** high, low, straight, receding, overhanging

9. **Brows:** straight, arched, winding-broad, narrow, knitted.

10. **Nose:** small, large--thick, thin, broad. Bridge of nose: concave, straight, pro-tuberant and hooked. Base of nose: raised, horizontal, lowered.

11. **Mouth:** small, large. Corners of mouth: lowered, raised.

12. **Lips:** thin, thick, hanging lower lip, raised upper.

13. **Chin:** receding, straight, protruding, double, dimpled, furrowed crosswise.

14. **Ears:** small, large-oval, triangular, square, round. Protuberance of ears: upper, lower, general. Earlobes: joined, separate, slanted, angular, oval.

16. Distinguishing features _Scar on the middle finger of the right_

physical abnormalities: mutilations, injuries;

hand on the first joint

additional features: growths, warts, extra fingers, spots, welts, scars, abnormal

body movements, baldness, assymetry of the face, different colored eyes, and others

tatooing (describe)

17. Other pecularities and habits _not noted_

gutturalizes "r'"s, stutters, bites nails,

various finger manipulations, gesticulates (indicate how), involuntary movements,

expectorates, spits, etc., etc.

18. When arrested _February 19_ 1949 warrant No. _536_

19. Basis for arrest _____

indicate name of document, organ, and date

20. Recorded with whom _Special section for the Division of Internal Affairs of the Ministry of State Security of the USSR_

Анкета заполнена *В приеме арестованных*
указать наименование тюрьмы или КПЗ
Внутренней тюрьмы МГБ СССР
Москвы

Город, село, ж.-д. ст. _____

Кем *Зам. Д. п. и. т. или Жидовилов*
должность, звание, фамилия

Подпись _____

Место для фотокарточки (арестованного)

Отпечаток указательного пальца
правой руки
(от одной кромки ногтя до другой)

ФОТОГРАФИРОВАН И ДАКТИЛОСКОПИРОВАН
в _____ МГБ. СССР

"21" II _____ 1949 года

Личная подпись *Каганович*
(арестованного)

Form filled out _____ *at the reception office for arrestees*
indicate name of prision or preliminary detention facility
_____ *of the Internal Prison of the USSR Ministry of State Security*

City, town, railroad station _____ *Moscow* _____

By whom *Dep. Dir.* [illegible] *of the prison   Zhidovikov*
position, title, last name

Signature _____ Zhidovikov _____

Place for photo (of the arrestee)

Print of the first finger
    of the right hand
(from one edge of the nail to the other)

| PHOTOGRAPHED AND FINGERPRINTED |
| **in the 1st Div. of Dep't A of the USSR MGB** | **Personal signature**
| _____ *Feb. 21* _____ 194 9 | **(of the arrestee)**

Kaganovich

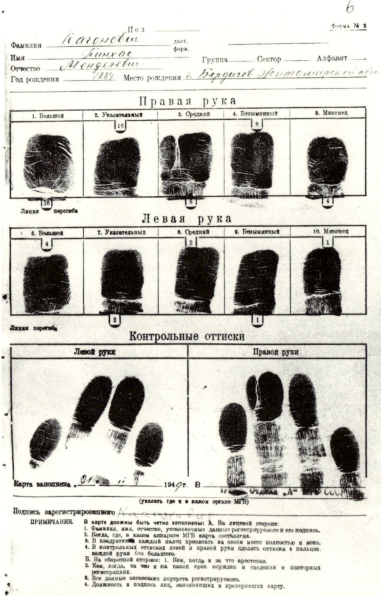

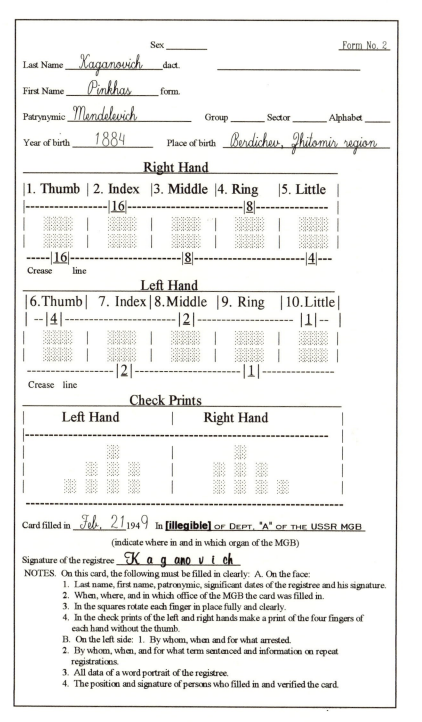

Sex _____   <u>Form No. 2</u>

Last Name _*Kaganovich*_ dact.   _____

First Name _*Pinkhas*_ form.

Patrynymic *Mendelevich*   Group _____ Sector _____ Alphabet _____

Year of birth _*1884*_   Place of birth *Berdichev, Zhitomir region*

Right Hand

1. Thumb	2. Index	3. Middle	4. Ring	5. Little
		16			8		

-----|16|--------------------|8|----------------------|4|---
Crease   line

Left Hand

6.Thumb	7. Index	8.Middle	9. Ring	10.Little
--|4|--		|2|	|1|--	

-------------------|2|--------------------|1|---------------
Crease   line

Check Prints

Left Hand		Right Hand	

Card filled in _*Feb. 21*_ 194 *9* In **[illegible]** OF DEPT. "A" OF THE USSR MGB

(indicate where in and in which organ of the MGB)

Signature of the registree _*K a g ano v i ch*_

NOTES. On this card, the following must be filled in clearly: A. On the face:
   1. Last name, first name, patronymic, significant dates of the registree and his signature.
   2. When, where, and in which office of the MGB the card was filled in.
   3. In the squares rotate each finger in place fully and clearly.
   4. In the check prints of the left and right hands make a print of the four fingers of each hand without the thumb.
   B. On the left side: 1. By whom, when and for what arrested.
   2. By whom, when, and for what term sentenced and information on repeat registrations.
   3. All data of a word portrait of the registree.
   4. The position and signature of persons who filled in and verified the card.

СЕКРЕТНО

МЕД-СПРАВКА

13 февраля 1949 г. осмотрен в 2 — тюрьме МГБ СССР

заключен. *Каганович Пинхиса*

Менделевич

Жалобы *[неразборчиво]*

Осмотром установлено:

- Температура тела _____
- Полость рта _____
- Кожа и слизистые _____
- Подкожно-жировой слой _____
- Наружные повреждения _____
- Венерические заболевания _____
- Внутренние органы _____
- Вшивость _____
- Заключение _____
- Санитарная обработка произведена _____ 19/II 49

Деж. врач _[подпись]_

Medical Certificate

Feb. 19 1949 there was examined in __[illegible]__ prison of the

USSR _M_ NKGB prisoner _____ Kaganovich Pinkhas

Mendelevich _____

Complaints _suffered from hemorrhoids, heart pain_

Findings of the Examination:

Body temperature _n_

Mouth cavity _clear pharynx_

Skin and mucous membrane _pale_

Subcutaneous fat layer _weakly developed_

External injuries _deformation of the chest_

Venereal diseases _no_ [illegible]

Internal organs _accented hard tones_

hemorrhoidal nodes

Pediculosis _none_

Conclusion _hemmorrhoid arteriocardiosclerosis_

malnutrition [?illegible]

Health processing done _____

Feb. 19, 1949 _____

Duty physician [Illegible signature]

———— час. ———— мин.

8

ПРОТОКОЛ

обыска заключенного *Когонович Пинхо*

Менделеевич прибывшего *19* "*февраля* 1949 г.

во Внутреннюю тюрьму МГБ из *г. Москва*

Обыску подвергнуты все личные вещи.

При обыске оказалось: *ничего не обнаружено*

Подпись заключенного *Каганович*

Обыск производил *Ротань*

При обыске присутствовал

Деж. пом. начальника Внутренней тюрьмы МГБ

"*19*" *февраля* 1949 г.

R E C O R D

___ hour ____ min.

of the search of prisoner ____*Kogonovich   Pinkhos*____

____*Mendeleevich*____ who arrived ____*February 19*____ 194*9*

at the Internal Prison of the MGB from ____*Moscow*____

All personal possessions have been subjected to search.

In the course of the search was found: ____*nothing was found*____

Signature of the prisoner ____*K a g a n o vich*____

Search done by ____*Rotkin*____

Present during the search _____

[Illegible signature]
Duty assistant of the head of the Internal Prison of the MGB

____*February 19*_____194*9*

СОВ. СЕКРЕТНО

ВНУТРЕННЯЯ ТЮРЬМА МГБ СССР
гор. Москва

"22/II"   1949 г.   № 201

СЛУЖЕБНАЯ ЗАПИСКА

Начальнику *Деф. Нач. Внутр. тюр.*

Капитану   тов. *Кузнецов*

Начальнику *Лефортовской тюр.*

Подполковнику   тов. *Попов*

Арестован. *Каганович*
Михаил Менделевич

Отправьте в *Лефортовскую тюр.*
Примите из *Внутренней тюр.*
и поместите *в камеру № 102 к арес.*
№ 45.

Изолировав от арестован.

Основание: *Указание Комит*

Арестованного числить за _____ *тюрьм*

[stamp]   Начальник внутренней тюрьмы МГБ СССР [signature]

Секретарь внутренней тюрьмы МГБ СССР [signature]

TOP SECRET

INTERNAL PRISON OF THE
USSR MINISTRY OF STATE SECURITY
Moscow

Feb. 22 194_9_   No. _207_

OFFICIAL RECORD

To the head _Duty Assistant to the Head of the Internal Prison_
Captain

_____ Comrade _Kuznetsov_

To the head _____ _of Lefortovo Prison_
Lieutenant Colonel

_____ Comrade __ _Ionov_

Arrestee _____ _Kaganovich_
_____ _Pinkhas Mendelevich_

Send to ___ _Lefortovo Prison_

Receive from ___ _Internal Prison_

and place _in Cell No. 102 to_ [illegible] _No._ 45

Isolated from arrestee _____

B a s i s: _Instruction_ [illegible]

Register the arrestee under _Investigation Section of the MGB_

| USSR | **Head of the Internal Prison of the USSR**
| Ministry| **Ministry of State Security**   _Kuznetsov_
| of state | **Secretary of the Internal Prision of the USSR**
|Security| **Ministry of State Security**
|for cer- | [illegible signature]
|tificates | [seal]
| 11 |

СЕКРЕТНО

МЕД-СПРАВКА

10

22 _февраля_ 1949 г. осмотрен в _Лефор_ тюрьме НКГБ СССР

заключен. _Каганович Юнихаса_

Менделевич

Жалобы _на боли в сердце, страдает геморроем._

Осмотром установлено:

Температура тела _____

Полость рта _все целый_

Кожа и слизистые _бледноваты_

Подкожно-жировой слой _слабо развит_

Наружные повреждения _деформация грудной клетки_

Венерические заболевания _наружных признаков нет._

Внутренние органы _тоны сердца акцентированы_
имеются геморроидальные узлы.

Вшивость _нет._

Заключение _артериокардиосклероз, геморрой,_
пониженное питание.

Санитарная обработка произведена _22.II.49_

Деж. врач _[подпись]_

Произведенные прививки _____

Medical Certificate

Feb. 22 1949 there was examined in __Lefortovo__ Prison of the USSR People's Commissariat of State Security prisoner _Kaganovich Pinkhas Mendelevich_

Complaints __pain in the heart; suffers from hemorrhoids__

Findings of the Examination:

Body temperature ___n___

Mouth cavity __clear pharynx__

Skin and mucous membrane __pale__

Subcutaneous fat layer __weakly developed__

External injuries __deformation of the chest__

Venereal diseases ___no external signs___

Internal organs __heart tones accented. Hemorrhoidal nodes__

Pediculosis ___none___

Conclusion __arteriocardiosclerosis, hemorrhoids, malnutrition__

Health processing done ___Feb. 22, 1949___

**Duty physician** [illegible signature]

Inoculations done _____

ПРОТОКОЛ

обыска заключенного _Каганович Пинхас_

Менделевич прибывшего _22/II_ 1949 г.

в _Лефортовскую_ тюрьму МГБ из _Бутырки_

_М.Г.Б._

Обыску подвергнуты все личные вещи.

При обыске оказалось: _ничего не обнаружено_

_____

Подпись заключенного _Каганович_

Обыск производил _Долгов_

При обыске присутствовал _Дмитриев_

Деж. пом. начальника _Лефортовской_ тюрьмы МГБ

_22/II_ 1949 г. _Белич_

___ hour ___ min.

RECORD

of the search of prisoner_____ *Kaganovich   Pinkhas* _____
_____ *Mendelevich* _____ who arrived_____ *February* 22 1949
at _*Lefortovo*_ prison of the Ministry of State Security from ___
_____ [illegible] *of the Ministry of State Security* _____

All personal possessions have been subjected to search.

In the course of the search was found: _*nothing was found*_

Signature of the prisoner ℜ **a g a ʀ o** vich _____
Search done by _____ *Dolgov* _____
Present during the search [illegible signature] _____

Duty assistant of the head of *Lefortovo* Prison of the Ministry of State Security

February 22 _____1949   [illegible signature]

ОТДЕЛ „А" МГБ СССР

СОВЕРШЕННО СЕКРЕТНО

тюрьмы МГБ СССР

Начальнику _____
подполковнику

тов. _____

Сообщаем, что арестованному

_____ Пагановиг

содержащемуся в _____ МГБ СССР, числящемуся

за _____ МГБ СССР

срок содержания под стражей продлен до „19" _____ 194__ года.

Начальник 1 отделения отдела „А" МГБ СССР
подполковник _____ Воробьев

ст. Оперуполномоченный _____

„6" __IV__ 194__ года.

№ 18/1 _____

2191

April 18, 1949 [illegible] **DEPARTMENT "A" OF THE USSR MGB**

TOP SECRET

To the head _____ Lieutenant Colonel _____ of Lefortovo _____ Prison of the USSR Ministry of State Security

Comrade _____ Sonov _____

We report that for detainee _____ Kaganovich _____

Pinkhos Mendelevich _____, who is held

at _____ Lefortovo Prison _____ of the USSR Ministry of State Security, and who is registered

under _____ Investigative Section of the Dep't of Internal Affairs of the USSR Ministry of State Security

the term of detention under guard is extended until _____ May 19 _____ 1949

Head of the First Division of Department "A" of the USSR MGB

_____ Lieutenant Colonel _____ Vorob'ev _____ Vorob'ev _____

Duty agent

Senior _____ Captain _____ Dubiia _____

| Entry No. 1079
| April 19 1949
| Lefortovo Prison of
| the USSR NKVD

No. 18/1 -- 2191
April 16 1949

13

ОТДЕЛ „А" МГБ СССР

СОВЕРШЕННО СЕКРЕТНО

Начальнику _Ленартелей_ _подполковнику_ тюрьмы МГБ СССР

тов. _иочому_

Гагановиг

Сообщаем, что арестованному _Тихоеу Мещелевигу_

в _Ленортелей тюе_ _____ МГБ СССР, содержащемуся

за _след. геекою по 0138_ _____ МГБ СССР, числящемуся

Срок содержания под стражей продлен до „19" июня 194 9 года.

Начальник 1 отделения отдела „А" МГБ СССР
подполковник _Воробев_

б) Оперуполномоченный _Дубев_
Кешргеи

Зак. № 1355
20.V 1949 г.
Печатная тип. НКВД СССР

№ 18/1— 2191

„18" V 19 49 года.

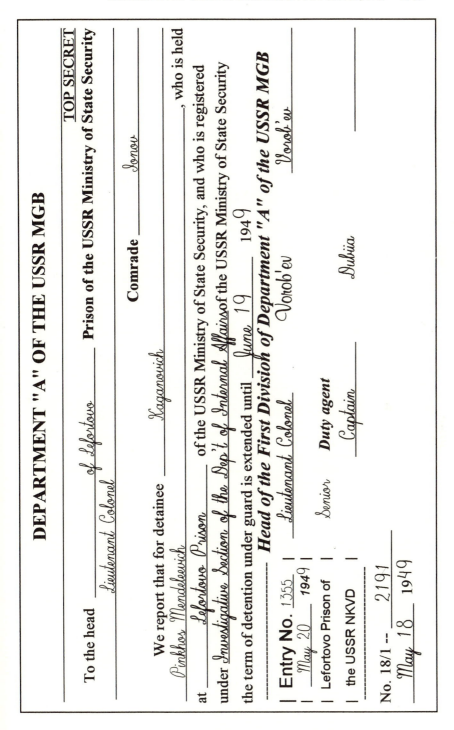

DEPARTMENT "A" OF THE USSR MGB

TOP SECRET

To the head _Lieutenant Colonel_ of _Lefortovo_ Prison of the USSR Ministry of State Security

Comrade _Sonov_

We report that for detainee _Kaganovich_

Pinkhos Mendeleevich , who is held

at _Lefortovo Prison_ of the USSR Ministry of State Security, and who is registered

under _Investigative Section of the Dep't of Internal Affairs_ of the USSR Ministry of State Security

the term of detention under guard is extended until _June 19_ 194_9_

Head of the First Division of Department "A" of the USSR MGB
Lieutenant Colonel _Vorob'ev_ _Vorob'ev_

Duty agent
Senior _Captain_ _Dubria_

| Entry No. 1355 |
| _May 20_ 1949 |
| Lefortovo Prison of |
| the USSR NKVD |

No. 18/1 -- 2191
May 18 1949

Г.к.2   С Е К Р Е Т Н О

14

З А К Л Ю Ч Е Н И Е

Заключенный КАГАНОВИЧ Пинхас Менделеевич, 1884 года рождения поступил в Лефортовскую тюрьму МГБ СССР с болями в области заднего прохода, кровотечение из геморроидальных узлов при акте дефикации, нарастающую общую слабость.

Об"ективно: заключенный бледен, резко истощен, в легких везикулярное дыхание, тоны сердца приглушени. Язык слегка обложен, влажен, живот мягкий, безболезненный при пальпации. В области заднего прохода имеется несколько воспаленных геморроидальных узлов наружных и внутренних. Так как заключенный каждый день теряет значительное количество крови у него продолжается нарастать малокровие, что в его возрасте, очень опасно.

Консервативные методы лечения не дают достаточных результатов.

Заключенного КАГАНОВИЧА необходимо показать квалифицированному хирургу для консультации и возможности оперативного лечения.

НАЧАЛЬНИК САНЧАСТИ ЛЕФОРТОВСКОЙ ТЮРЬМЫ
МГБ СССР - Подполковник медслужбы -

                                               (ЯНШИН)

" 4 " июля 1949 года

g.k.2   S E C R E T

C O N C L U S I O N

Prisoner Pinkhas Mendeleevich KAGANOVICH born
in 1884, arrived at Lefortovo Prison of the USSR
MGB with pains in the area of the rectum, bleeding
from hemorrhoidal nodes during the act of
defecation, with a growing general weakness.

Objectively: the prisoner is pale, sharply
emaciated, vesicular breathing in the lungs,
muffled heartbeats. The tongue is lightly coated
and moist, the abdomen soft, not painful to
palpitation. In the area of the rectum there are a
number of inflamed external and internal
hemorrhoidal nodes. Since the prisoner each day
loses a significant quantity of blood, his anemia
is continuing to increase, which, at his age, is
very dangerous.

Conservative methods of treatment are not
giving adequate results.

Prisoner KAGANOVICH must be shown to a
qualified surgeon for consultation and the
possibility of treatment by an operation.

HEAD OF THE HEALTH SECTION OF LEFORTOVO PRISON OF
THE USSR MGB - Lt.Colonel of the Medical Service

                    Ianshin   (Ianshin)

July 4 , 1949

З.л.2.

Лефортовская тюрьма
июля 49
в 3 ч

Отпеч. 2 экз.
1—адресату
2—в дело

НАЧАЛЬНИКУ СЛЕДЧАСТИ ПО ОСОБО-ВАЖНЫМ ДЕЛАМ
МГБ СССР - Генерал-майору -
тов. Л Е О Н О В У.-

При этом препровождается заключение вра-
ча тюрьмы о состоянии здоровья заключенного
КАГАНОВИЧА Пинхаса Менделеевича - для
сведения.

ПРИЛОЖЕНИЕ: упомянутое.-

НАЧАЛЬНИК ЛЕФОРТОВСКОЙ ТЮРЬМЫ МГБ СССР
Подполковник -   /ИОНОВ/

С Е К Р Е Т А Р Ь ТЮРЬМЫ
Майор -   /КАЛИНИН/

z.1.2.

D/3

TO THE HEAD OF THE INVESTIGATION SECTION OF THE USSR MGB
FOR ESPECIALLY IMPORTANT CASES - Major General -

Comrade LEONOV -

Lefortovo Prison

July 4 49

No. 3027

Herewith is forwarded the conclusion of the
prison's physician on the state of health of
the prisoner Pinkhas Mendeleevich KAGANOVICH,
- for information.

2 copies typed.
1 - for the addressee
2 - to the file

ATTACHMENT: aforementioned.-

HEAD OF LEFORTOVO PRISON OF THE USSR MGB
Lieutenant -   /IONOV/

SECRETARY   OF THE PRISON
Major -

Malinin /MALININ/

16

ОТДЕЛ „А" МГБ СССР

СОВЕРШЕННО СЕКРЕТНО

Начальнику _Федоровской_ _подполковнику_ тюрьмы МГБ СССР

тов. _Чонову_

Сообщаем, что арестованному _Каганович_ _Пинхосу Менделевичу_ содержащемуся _Федоровской тюрьме_ МГБ СССР, числящемуся _за по Особо-Важным Делам_ МГБ СССР

срок содержания под стражей продлен до "19" VIII 1949 года.

Начальник 1 отделения отдела „А" МГБ СССР И. _Оробо_ (Воробьёв)

подполковник

Оперуполномоченный _Капитон_ _Лешенира_

Вх. № 2110
"6." VI 194 г
Федоровск тюрьмы НКВД СССР

№ 18/1- 2191

"15." VII 1949 года.

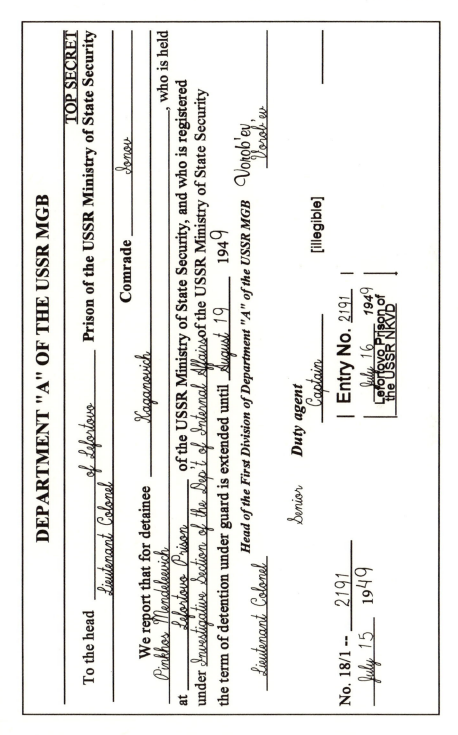

DEPARTMENT "A" OF THE USSR MGB

TOP SECRET

To the head _Lieutenant Colonel_ of _Lefortovo_ Prison of the USSR Ministry of State Security

Comrade _Sorov_

We report that for detainee _Pinkhos Mendeleevich Kaganovich_, who is held at _Lefortovo Prison_ of the USSR Ministry of State Security, and who is registered under _Investigative Section of the Dep't of Internal Affairs_ of the USSR Ministry of State Security the term of detention under guard is extended until _August 19_ 19_49_

Head of the First Division of Department "A" of the USSR MGB _Vorob'ev_

Lieutenant Colonel _Vorob'ev_

Duty agent _Senior_ _Captain_ [illegible]

| Entry No. 2191

July 16 1949

Lefortovo Prison of the USSR NKVD

No. 18/1 -- 2191

July 15 1949

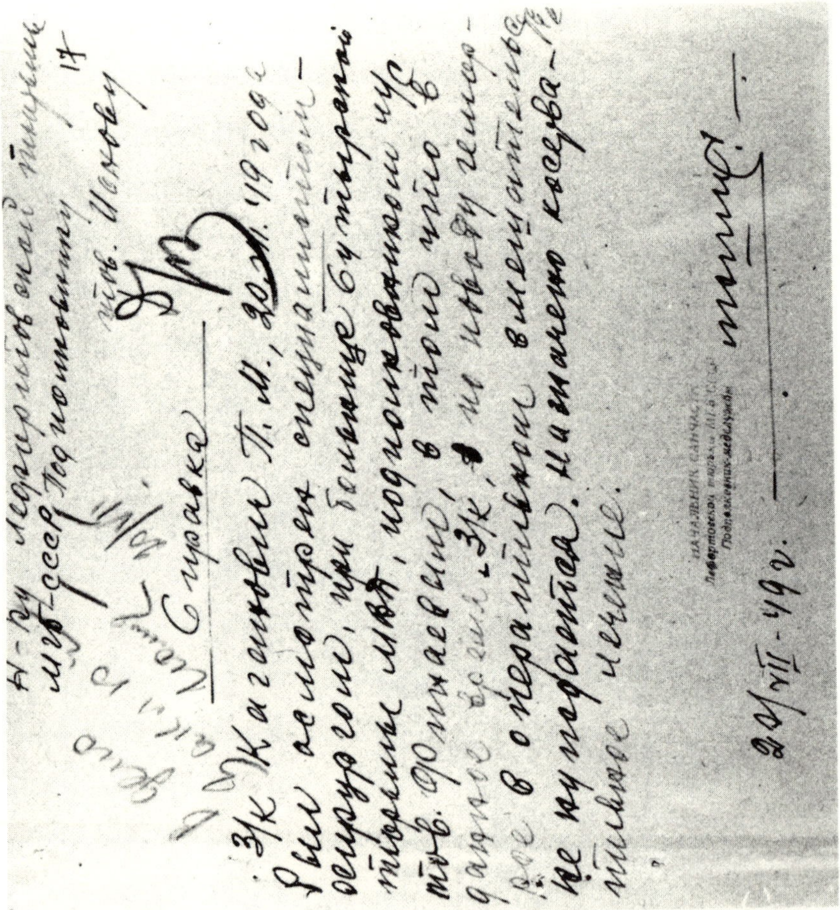

Н-ку Лефортовской тюрьмы
МГБ-СССР Подполковнику
тов. Ионову
17

В дело
Заключ.
20/VII

Справка

З/к Каганович П. М., 20.VII.49 года был осмотрен специалистом-хирургом, при больнице Бутырской тюрьмы МВД, подполковником м/с тов. Фомичевым, в том что в данное время З/к, по поводу геморроя в оперативном вмешательстве не нуждается. Назначено консервативное лечение.

НАЧАЛЬНИК САНЧАСТИ
Лефортовской тюрьмы МГБ СССР
Подполковник-медслужбы

21/VII-49 г.

To the Head of Lefortovo Prison of the USSR MGB, Lieutenant Colonel

Comrade Jonov

Comrade Jonov July 20

Include in file

Note

Prisoner Kaganovich, P.M., on July 20, 1949, was examined by a surgical specialist attached to the hospital of Butyrka Prison of the MVD, Lieutenant Colonel of the Medical Service Comrade Finaev, to the effect that at the present time the prisoner, with respect to his hemorrhoids does not need operative intervention. Conservative treatment has been prescribed.

HEAD OF THE HEALTH SECTION
of Lefortovo Prison of the USSR MGB
Lieutenant Colonel of the Medical Service

[Illegible signature]

July 27, 1949

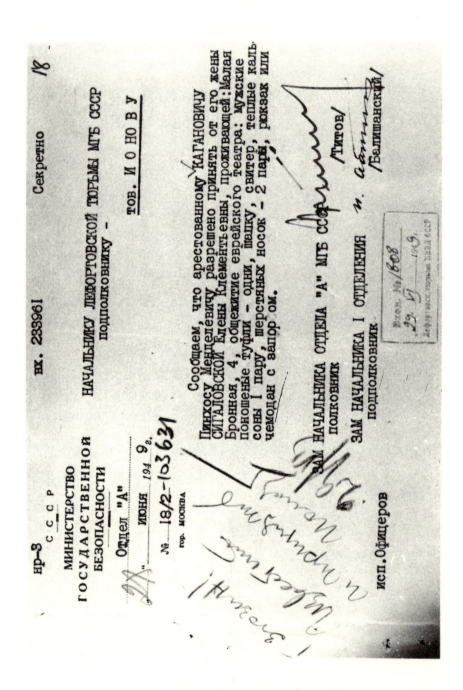

нр-3

СССР

МИНИСТЕРСТВО
ГОСУДАРСТВЕННОЙ
БЕЗОПАСНОСТИ

Отдел "А"

"___" ИЮНЯ 194 9 г.

№ 18/2-103631

гор. МОСКВА

вх. 233961   Секретно   18

НАЧАЛЬНИКУ ЛЕФОРТОВСКОЙ ТЮРЬМЫ МГБ СССР
подполковнику -

тов. И О Н О В У

Сообщаем, что арестованному КАГАНОВИЧУ Пинхосу Менделевичу разрешено принять от его жены СИГАЛОВСКОЙ Елены Клементьевны, проживающей: Бронная, 4, общежитие еврейского театра: мужские поношенные туфли - одни, шапку, свитер, теплые кальсоны 1 пару, шерстяных носок - 2 пары, пиджак или чемодан с запором.

ЗАМ НАЧАЛЬНИКА ОТДЕЛА "А" МГБ СССР
полковник /Титов/

ЗАМ НАЧАЛЬНИКА I ОТДЕЛЕНИЯ
подполковник /Белишанский/

исп.Офицеров

no.-3   entry 233961   Secret

U S S R

MINISTRY
OF STATE
SECURITY   TO THE HEAD OF LEFORTOVO PRISON OF THE USSR

Lieutenant Colonel -

       Comrade I o n o v

Department "A"

June 28 1949

No. 18-2-103631

MOSCOW

    We report that arrestee Pinkhos Mendelevich KAGANOVICH is permitted
to receive from his wife Elena Klement'evna SIGALOVSKAIA, residing at
the Dormitory of the Jewish Theater, Malaia Bronnaia 4: worn men's
slippers - one pair, a cap, a sweater, warm long underwear - 1 pair,
wool socks - 2 pair, a backpack or suitcase with a lock.

*Comrade J.gin!
I have notified and
it has been received.
June 29 – Jonov*

DEPUTY HEAD OF DEPARTMENT "A" OF THE USSR MGB
    Colonel   *Titov* /Titov/

DEPUTY HEAD OF THE FIRST DIVISION
    Lt. Colonel   *J. Balishanskii* /Balishanskii/
of the administering officers

| Entry No. 1808 |
| June 29 1949 |
| Lefortovo Prison of |
| the USSR NKVD |

ОТДЕЛ „А" МГБ СССР

19

СОВЕРШЕННО СЕКРЕТНО

Начальнику _Лефортовской_ _____ тюрьмы МГБ СССР
подполковнику

тов. _Ионову_

Сообщаем, что арестованному _Кагановичу Пинхосу_
Менделевичу содержащемуся

в _Лефортовской тюрьме_ _____ МГБ СССР, числящемуся

за _4/2 по Особо Важным Делам_ МГБ СССР

срок содержания под стражей продлен до _19_ . _VII_ 194_9_ года.

Зам Начальник 1 отделения отдела „А" МГБ СССР
подполковник _И. Ог. (барашкова)_

Оперуполномоченный
Капитан Аникина

Вход № 15** _____
16 июня 19

№ 18/1 — 2191
15 . VI . 194_9_ года.

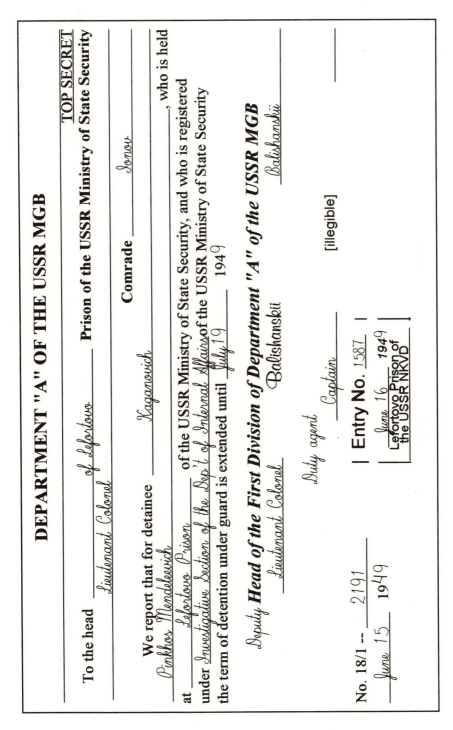

DEPARTMENT "A" OF THE USSR MGB

TOP SECRET

To the head _Lieutenant Colonel_ of _Lefortovo_ Prison of the USSR Ministry of State Security

Comrade _Sorov_

We report that for detainee _Kaganovich_

Pinkhos Mendelevich, who is held

at _Lefortovo Prison_ of the USSR Ministry of State Security, and who is registered

under _Investigative Section of the Dep't of Internal Affairs_ of the USSR Ministry of State Security

the term of detention under guard is extended until _July 19_ _1949_

Deputy **_Head of the First Division of Department "A" of the USSR MGB_**

Lieutenant Colonel _Balishanskii_ _Balishanskii_

Duty agent

Captain [illegible]

Entry No. 1587

June 16 1949
Lefortovo Prison of
the USSR NKVD

No. 18/1 -- 2191
June 15 1949

20

ОРДЕР № 2191

Начальнику _Лефортовской_ Тюрьмы МГБ СССР

г. Москва

Арестованного _Каганович_

Пинхас Менделеевич

год рождения _1884_

перечислите содержанием за _____

особ. совещ. при мгб ссср куда

"___" _____ 194_ г. ___

отправлено его дело № _2191_ для ___

рассмотрения

О перечислении объявите арестованному под расписку на обороте сего и сообщите нам талоном ордера.

Зам. Начальник отдела "А"
МГБ СССР

Начальник 1 отделения

"_5_" _x_ ___ 19__ г.

2976

6   x
9

Лефортовск. тюрьма НКВД СССР

TOP SECRET

Comrade **[illegible]**

Transferred

October 6, 1949 **[illegible]**

ORDER No. 2191

To the head of *Lefortovo* **prison of the USSR MGB**

Moscow

Arrestee _____ *Kaganovich* _____

Pinkhas Mendeleevich _____

_____ born in ___ 1884 ___

is to be reassigned to custody for _____

_____ *the Special Board attached to the USSR MGB* ___ to which

on _____ 194 _____

his file No. 2191 was sent for _____

_____ *consideration* _____

Notify the arrestee of the reassignment against his signature on reverse hereof and inform us with the coupon of the order.

Deputy **Head of Department "A"** [illegible signature]

of the USSR MGB

Head of the First Division [illegible signature]

October 5 194 9

| Entry No. 2976
| _Oct. 6_ 1949
| Lefortovo Prison of
| the USSR NKVD

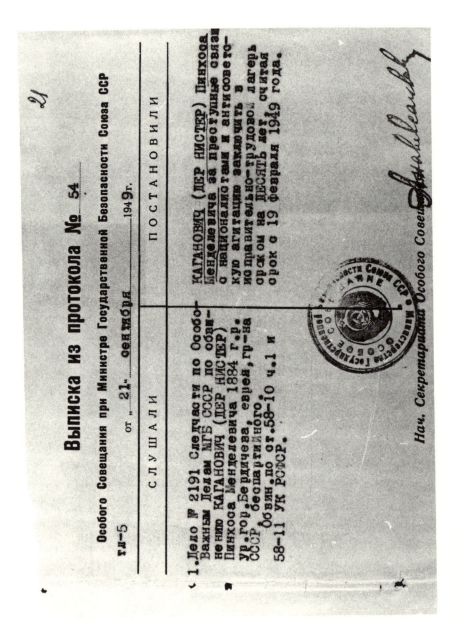

2

Выписка из протокола № 54

Особого Совещания при Министре Государственной Безопасности Союза ССР

тл-5   от "21" сентября 1949 г.

СЛУШАЛИ	ПОСТАНОВИЛИ
1.Дело № 2191 Следчасти по Особо-Важным Делам МГБ СССР по обви-нению КАГАНОВИЧ (ДЕР НИСТЕР) Пинхоса Менделевича 1884 г.р. ур.гор.Бердичева, еврей, гр-на СССР беспартийного. Обвин.по от.58-10 ч.1 и 58-11 УК РСФСР.	КАГАНОВИЧ (ДЕР НИСТЕР) Пинхоса Менделевича за преступные связи с националистами и антисоветс-кую агитацию заключить в исправительно-трудовой лагерь сроком на ДЕСЯТЬ лет считая срок с 19 февраля 1949 года.

Нач. Секретариата Особого Совещания

Excerpt from Record No. 54

Of the Special Board attached to the Ministry of State Security of the USSR

t1-5   of September 21   194 9

HEARD	DECIDED
1. Case No. 2191 of the Investigation Section for Especially Important Cases of the USSR Ministry of State Security on the accusation against Pinkhos Medelevich KAGANOVICH (DER NISTER), born in 1884, native of the city of Berdichev, Jew, not a party member. Accused under Art. 58-10 pt 1 pt. 1 and 58 11 of the RSFSR Criminal Code.	To confine Pinkhos Mendelevich KAGANOVICH (DER NISTER), for criminal ties with nationalists and for anti-Soviet propagandizing, to a corrective labor camp for a term of TEN years, calculating the term from February 19, 1949.

[MGB Special Board Seal]

22

СССР

**МИНИСТЕРСТВО
ВНУТРЕННИХ ДЕЛ**

Главное управление исправительно-
трудовых лагерей и колоний

2-е Управление

г. Москва

Наряд приобщается к личному делу осуж-
денного и является основанием к отправке
его в ЛАГЕРЬ, указанный в данном наряде.

СЕКРЕТНО

НАРЯД № 9/со-48070

Осуждён. *Особ. сов. при МГБ СССР*

21. IX. 194 *9* г.

по ст.ст. *58-10 ч. I, 58-11*

сроком на *10* лет. Содержан. в тюрьме *Лефортовск.*

города *Москва*

Каганович (Дернштейн) Пинхас
Менделевич   *1884* года рождения,
(фамилия, имя, отчество)

состояние здоровья и трудоспособность *годен к легк. физ.*
труду

Специальность *писатель*

направьте для отбытия срока наказания в *минеральный* ЛАГЕРЬ

на ст. *Абезь Печер. ж.д.*

Начальник 2 Управления
ГУЛАГа МВД СССР
Зам.
Капитан   (*Шедрин*)

Начальник « *4* » отделения
Ст. л-нт   (*Крылов*)

« *14* » *X*   194 *9* г.

(особые условия наряда см. на обороте)

USSR
---=---
**MINISTRY
OF INTERNAL AFFAIRS**
---=---
**Main Administration of Corrective
Labor Camps and Colonies
2nd Administration**

This order is included in the personal file of the convict and is the basis for sending him to the **CAMP** indicated in the present order.

SECRET

Moscow   **ORDER No. 9/so-**48070

Convicted by _the Special Board Attached to the USSR Ministry_ _of State Security_ _September 21,_ 194 9

under Articles _58-10 pt. 1, 58-11_

to a term of _10_ years. Confined in _Lefortovo_ prison

in the city of _Moscow_

Kaganovich (Dernister) Pinkhas
(last name, first name, patronymic)

Mendelevich

born in _1884_ ,

condition of health and ability to work _fit for light physical labor_

_____ **Specialty** _writer_

is to be sent to serve the term of punishment to _Mineral'nyi_ **CAMP**

at _Abez'_ Station on the _Pecherskaia Railroad_

[illegible]

**Head of the 2nd Administration
of the Main Administration of Camps
of the USSR Ministry of Internal Affairs**

Deputy

Captain   [illegible signature]   (_Shchedrin_)

Head of the _4th_ **Department**

Senior Lieutenant   [illegible signature]   (_Krylov_)

October 14 194 9

(for special conditions of this order see the back)

FRONT

КП-4

"УТВЕРЖДАЮ"

ЗАМ НАЧ СЛЕДЧАСТИ ПО ОСОБО ВАЖ-
НЫМ ДЕЛАМ МГБ СССР – Полковник

(КОМАРОВ)

" 17 " августа 1949 года.

ПОСТАНОВЛЕНИЕ

(о направлении в особый лагерь)

Гор.Москва, 1949 года, августа " 17 " дня.

Я, ст.следователь Следчасти по особо важным делам
МГБ СССР, подполковник ЦВЕТАЕВ, рассмотрев материалы следственного дела № 2191 по обвинению КАГАНОВИЧА (дер Нистера)
Пинхоса Менделеевича в совершении преступлений, предусмотренных ст.58-10 ч.I и 58-II УК РСФСР,–

НАШЕЛ:

Следствием по делу установлено, что КАГАНОВИЧ на про-
тяжении ряда лет проводил вражескую националистическую
деятельность и по своей преступной работе был связан с
особо-опасными государственными преступниками.

Принимая во внимание изложенное,–

BACK

ПОСТАНОВИЛ:

Направить КАГАНОВИЧА (дер Нистера) Пинхоса Менделеевича в особый лагерь МВД СССР.

СТ СЛЕДОВАТЕЛЬ СЛЕДЧАСТИ ПО ОСОБО ВАЖНЫМ
ДЕЛАМ МГБ СССР – Подполковник

(ЦВЕТАЕВ)

FRONT

kp-4

"I APPROVE"

DEPUTY HEAD OF THE INVESTIGATION
SECTION FOR ESPECIALLY IMPORTANT
CASES OF THE USSR MINISTRY OF
INTERNAL AFFAIRS -- Colonel
                              (KOMAROV)

August 17 1949

DECISION
==========

(to send to a special camp)

Moscow, August 17 1949

I, Senior Investigator of the Investigation
Division for Particularly Important Cases of the USSR
Ministry of Internal Affairs, Lieutenant Colonel
TSVETAEV, having considered the materials of the
investigation of Case No. 2191 on the accusation
against Pinkhas Mendeleevich KAGANOVICH (Der Nister)
of commission of the crimes defined in Articles 58-
10, pt. 1, and 58-11 of the Criminal Code of the
RSFSR.

                     I HAVE DETERMINED:
The investigation of the case has established
that KAGANOVICH for a period of years conducted
hostile nationalistic activity and in his criminal
work was involved with especially dangerous state
              criminals.

Taking the aforesaid into consideration, --

BACK

2.

           I HAVE DECIDED:
To send Pinkhas Mendeevich KAGANOVICH (Der Nister)
to a special camp of the Ministry of Internal Affairs
of the USSR.

SENIOR INVESTIGATOR OF THE INVESTIGATION
     SECTION FOR ESPECIALLY DANGEROUS CRIMES
     OF THE USSR MINISTRY OF INTERNAL

     AFFAIRS -- Lieutenant Colonel   *E. Tsvetaev*
                                        (Tsvetaev)

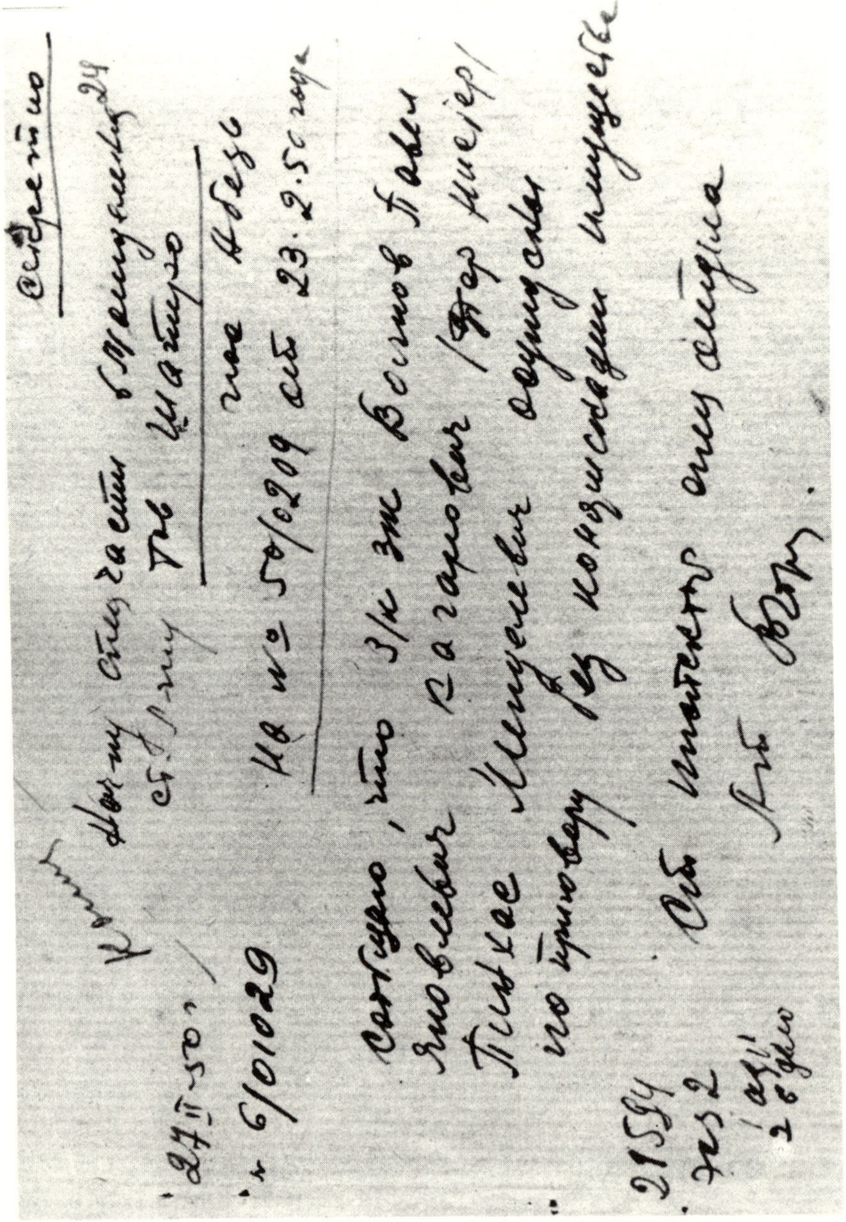

Секретно

Копия

Нач-у Спецчасти в Минлаге 24
ст. л-ту тов Шатрову
пос Абезь

27.II.50 г.
№ 6/01029

На № 50/0209 от 23.2.50 года

Сообщаю, что з/к эт Волгнов Павел Яковлевич Каганович /пер инженер/ Пинхас Менделевич осуждены по приговору без конфискации имущества

21594
экз 2
1 адр.
2 в дело

Ст инспектор спец отдела
Ст л-т Егоров.

copy   secret

To the head of the Special Section [illegible]

Senior Lieutenant Comrade Shapiro

Feb. 27, 1950   Aleg'

No. 6/01029   With respect to No. 50/0209 of Feb. 23, 1950

I report that prisoners [illegible] Pavel Jakovlevich Volkov, Pinkhas Mendelevich

Kaganovich /Der Nister/ have been convicted with a sentence without confiscation of

property.

21594

cop. 2   Senior Inspector of the Special Department

1 adm

2 to the file   [illegible signature]

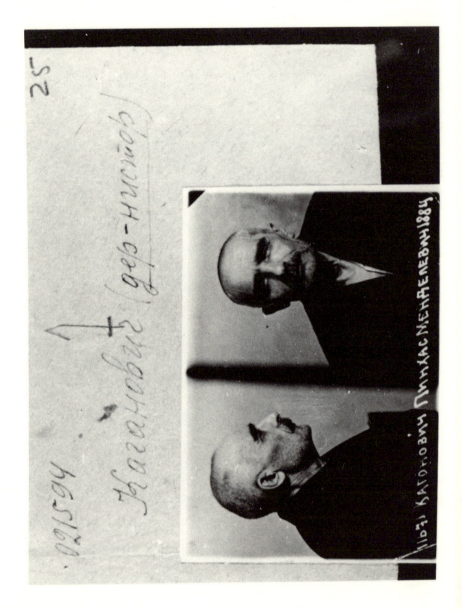

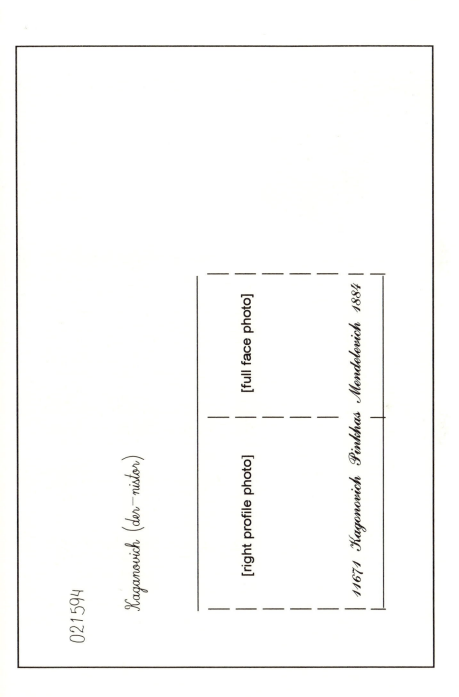

021594

Kaganovich (der-nister)

[right profile photo]   [full face photo]

11671 Kaganovich Pinkhus Mendelevich 1884

Киев 16/XI 99

Приложение № 3 к приказу
№ 0203—1940 г.

ТЮ... ... ...рокий

СПРАВКА

2б

Личный номер обыскиваемого

Лефортовская тюрьма МГБ СССР

М. П.

Справка по личному делу № 188/24

на заключенного   КАГАНОВИЧ

Пинхас Менделевич, он же ДЕР-НИС-

ТЕР Пинхас.

1. Год рождения 1884	2. Специальность **писатель**
3. Пункт назначения: город, селение, область, ж. д. станция, пристань. Через какие обменные пункты	**от. Абезь, Печорской жел. дороги**
4. В чье распоряжение следует (в какой лагерь, тюрьму, орган МВД, милиции)	**в распоряжение начальника МИНЕРАЛЬ-НОГО ЛАГЕРЯ МВД.**
5. Основание к отправке (наряд, распоряжение и т. д.)	**задание отдела "А" МГБ СССР № 2191 от 15/X-49г. и наряд ГУЛАГ'а МВД СССР № 9/СО-48070 от 14/X-49 года.**
6. Подследственный, осужденный или ссыльный	**осужденный**
7. Каким судебным органом, когда, по какой ст. УК и на какой срок осужден	**21/IX-49г. Особым Совещанием при МГБ СССР по ст. 58-10 ч.1, 58-11 УК РСФСР на 10 лет ИТЛ.**
8. Вид конвоя: обыкновенный, усиленный, мотивы:	**усиленный**
9. Особые приметы заключенного	**шрам на среднем пальце правой руки.**
10. Отметки врача: а) о состоянии здоровья заключ.	**Здоров, следовать может.**
б) о прохождении санобработки	**Санобработку прошел.** Подпись врача
в) о санитарном благополуч. т-мы	**Эпидемич. заболев. в тюрьме не было.**
11. Отметки о вложении дактилоскопической карты	**есть**

Начальник Лефортовской тюрьмы МГБ СССР

полковник-   (ИОНОВ)

[illegible] *Nov. 16, 1949* *Attachment No. 3 to order*
No. 0203-1940

PRISON No.   or'ki [partially illegible]

RECORD

No. [illegible]	Personal number of the person searched _____
Name [? partially illegible]	Lefortovo Prison of the USSR MGB
	Note for personal file No. 188/24
[partially illegible]	for the prisoner Pinkhas Mendelevich Kaganovich,
	also known as Pinkhas DER-NISTER .
|Place for Seal|	
1. Year of Birth ___1884___	2. Occupation ___writer___
3. Destination: city, settlement, region railroad station, wharf. Through which exchange points	Abez' Station, Pechorskaia RR
4. Traveling to whose disposition (to which camp, prison, agency of the MVD, police)	to the disposition of the Head of the of the MINERAL'NYI CAMP of the MVD
5. Bases for sending (order, decision, etc.)	assignment of Dep't "A" of the MGB No. 2191 of Oct. 15, 1949 and order of the USSR MVD GULAG No. 9/SO-48070 of Oct. 14, 1949
6. Under investigation, convict, or exile	convict
7. Sentenced by which judicial body, when, under which Article of the Criminal Code, to what term	Sept. 21,'49 by Special Board attached to the USSR MGB under Art. 58-10, pt. 1 and 58-11 of the RSFSR Criminal Code to 10 Years in a Corrective Labor Camp
8. Type of convoy: ordinary or reinforced, motives:	reinforced
9. Special features of the prisoner	scar on middle finger of the right hand.
10. Physician's remarks: a) on the prisoner's state of heath	Healthy, may travel
b) on undergoing physical examination	Passed physical exam | Physician's signature
c) on the health situation in the prison	There were no epidemic | *Grom*[partially illegible] illnesses in the prison
11. Remarks on enclosure of a fingerprint card	enclosed

[illegible seal]

Head of Lefortovo Prison of the USSR MGB *Ionov*
lieutenant -   (Ionov)

Форма № 1

Место для фотокарточки	_Название лагеря-колонии МВД_

ФОРМУЛЯР ЛИЧНОГО ДЕЛА № 021594.   27

Раздел I.

1. Фамилия _____ Калинович (Дон нистери)

2. Имя и отчество _____ Менделевич

3. Год и место рождения 1884г. г. Бердичев

4. Образование _____

5. Национальность _____ еврей

6. Гражданство _____ СССР

7. Бывш. партийность _____ б/п

8. Профессия _____

9. Специальность _____ писатель

10. Воен. специальность и звание _____

11. Занимаемая до осуждения должность _____ писатель нач. отд.

12. Местожительство до ареста Москва, ул. М-Горького д. 4

13. Осужден Особ. совещ. _____ МГБ СССР
название судебного органа

14. Когда 21.07.49 по ст. УК 58-10, 58-11 на срок 10 лет.

15. Начало срока 19 февраля 1949 конец срока 19 февраля 1959

16. Дополнительная мера наказания _____ нет

17. Прежние судимости _____ нет

Место печати   Нач. л-отделения (ИТК), п-пункта

Нач. УРЧ

Раздел II.

Приметы:

Рост _____

Телосложение _____

Цвет волос _____

Глаза _____ карие

Нос _____

Особые приметы _____

Дакто-оттиск большого пальца правой руки

Инспектор УРЧ _____ Кур...

Checked [illegible signature]

Feb. 9[?], 1950   Form No. 1

| Place for |
| photo |

Mineral'nyi Camp of the Ministry of Internal Affairs

name of Ministry of Internal Affairs camp-colony

PERSONAL FILE FORM No. ___021594.___

Section I.

1. Last name ___Kaganovich (Der Nister)___

2. First name and patronymic ___Pinkhas Mendelevich___

3. Year and place of birth ___1884 Berdichev___

4. Education ___home___

5. Nationality ___Jew___

6. Citizenship ___USSR___

7. Former party membership ___none___

8. Occupation ___

9. Specialty ___writer___

10. Military specialty and rank ___

11. Position occupied before conviction ___writer at home___

12. Residence before arrest ___4 Malaia Bronnaia St., Moscow___

13. Convicted by ___Special Board Attached to the USSR Ministry of Internal Affairs___

14. When ___Sept. 21, 1949___ under Crim. Code Art.___58-10pt1 58-11___for a ___10___ year term.

15. Start of term ___February 19, 1949___   End of term ___February 19, 1959___

16. Supplementary measure of punishment ___none___

17. Prior criminal record ___none___

Place   *Head of the Camp Division (Corrective Labor Colony), location* ___
for seal   *Head of the Records-Assignment Section*___

Section II.
Features:

Height ___average___

Build ___average___

Hair Color ___greying___

Eyes ___hazel___

Nose ___broad___

Distinguishing Features ___scar___
on the middle finger of the right
hand on the first joint___

**Fingerprint of the
right thumb**

Inspector of the Records-Assignment Section ___Kun[illegible]___

Раздел III.   Отметки о движении

Название лагпозразделения-колонии	Дата прибытия	Дата убытия	Примечание
6 л/о ли - 1	1/XII -49		

Раздел IV.   Изменение срока наказания

Дата	Название судебного органа	Изменение срока наказания	Новый конец срока	Расписка закл. об объявлении намёнен. срока наказания	Подпись писпевтора

Section III.   **Notes on movement**

Name of camp subdivision-colony	Date of arrival	Date of departure	Comments
Camp division 6, camp subdivision 1	Dec. 1, 1949		

Section IV.   **Change of the Term of Punishment**

Date	Name of judicial body	Change term of punish-	New end of term	Receipt for decision on declaration of a change of term of punishment	Signature of inspector

28

Раздел V.   **Взыскания и поощрения**

Наименование М. З.	Дата и № приказа, постановления	Какое взыскание-поощрение	За что конкретно	Дата направления к л-делу выписки из прик.-постанов.	Подпись инспектора

Раздел VI.   **Заключение квалифицированной комиссии**

Наименование М. З.	Дата и № протокола	Специальность-квалификация	Подпись члена квалификацион. комиссии или работника учета

Section V. **Penalties and Rewards**

Name of the the place of of detenion	Date & No. of order or decision	What penalty or reward	For what specifi- cally	Date sent to personal file; excerpts from order-decision	Signature of inspector

Section VI. **Conclusions of the Skill Evaluation Commission**

Name of place of detention	Date & No. of protocol	Specialty - skill	Signature of member of the Skill Evaluation Commision or Recordkeeping employee

Раздел VII. Результаты медосвидетельствования

Дата	Диагноз болезни	Категория общей трудоспособности	Категория трудоспособности по специальности	Подпись врача
		Инвалид		

Состоит на учете:

венерик

малярик

психозный

эпилептик

трахома

пеллагра

Section VII.   **Results of Medical Examination**

	Diagnosis of illness	Category of general ability	Category of ability to work by specialty	Physician's Signature
Jan. 21, 1950		disabled –	[illegible diagnosis]	[illegible signature]
Apr. 29, 1950		disabled		[same illegible signature]
May 7 1950	§24	Disabled	[illegible]	[different illegible signature]

Subject to Reporting

|venereal
|malarial
|psychotic
|epileptic
|trachoma
|pellagra

Акт о смерти   29

1950 года июня мца 4го дня мы, нижеподписавшиеся, Нач. Ц. Больницы

врач Смирнова М. Н.

Главный врач Верховин Н. И.

Лечащий врач Марковский В. А.

дежурный надзиратель Новожилов Н. Ф.

составили сей в том что 4го дня июня мца 1950 г. в 18 час. 00 мин. в Ц. Больнице корпус № 1 умер КОГАНОВИЧ Никлос Исаевич 1884 года рождения, ст. 58-11 срок 10 л. ср. в 19— 50 году по национальности еврей

Уроженец ... г. Берлин.

Диагноз: Геморрой, выпадение прямой кишки. Артерио-кардиосклероз. Декомп. мембранный порок сердца. Сепсис. Кахексия.

Причина смерти нарастающая недостаточность сердечной деятельности.

Нач. Ц. Больницы врач   /Смирнова/

Главный врач   /Верховин/

Лечащий врач   /Марковский/

дежурный надзиратель   /Новожилов/

Certificate of Death

On June 4, 1950, we, the undersigned,

    Head of the Central Hospital

    physician M.N. Smirnova

    Head physician N.I Perkhovna

    Treating physician V.A. Markovskii

Duty guard N.F. Novozhilov

have prepared this report to the effect that on the **4th** day of the month of June **1950** at 18 hours and 00 minutes in the Central Hospital, Block 1, there died Kaganovich Pinkhos Mendeleevich born 1884 art 58-11 term 10 end of term on 19/11/50, by nationality Jew

Native of

Berdichev

Diagnosis: Hemorrhoids, inflamation of the colon. Arterio-cardiosclerosis. Decomp. mitral defect of the heart. Sepsis. Cahepsia.

Cause of death *growing inadequacy of heart activity*

Head of the Central Hospital, physician   /Smirnova/

    Head physician   **[illegible signature]**   /Perkhovna/

    Treating physician   **[illegible signature]** /Markovkskii/

    Duty guard   Novozhilov

Акт о погребении   30

1950 года Июля меся, дня, мы, нижеподписавшиеся, представители:

Надзорслужбы Ляшенова Н.И.

Спецчасти —

И. Больницы Свалова

составили настоящий акт в том, что сего числа в 20 часов Утра на кладбище под Лит. Б произвели погребение трупа гр. Кагана заслуж. Петар. Кальман Мендилевич 1887 года рожд. статья 58-1-а врач 10 ч.ср. 1952. По национальности Еврей Уроженец г. Бердичев

Умерший в И.Больнице в корп. №1 Июля меся, 4 дня 1950 года в 13 ч. ... Труп доставленный с Лит. 1. на место погребения одет в нижнем белье уложен в деревянный гроб на левой ноге умершего привязана дощечка с надписью фамилия, имя, отчество, на могиле поставлен столбик с надписью Литер №Б-4.

Участвовавшие Надзорслужбы — ...
в погребении Спецчасти
представители И. Больницы

... ... 1950 года

Certificate of Burial

On June 7, 1950, we, the undersigned representatives:

Of the guard service   P.I. Alimova

Of the Special section

Of the Central Hospital   Svalovia

have prepared the present certificate to the effect that on this day, at   20

hours 00 minutes at the cemetery

under the Letter B we have conducted the burial of the body of

Prisoner Kaganovich (der Nister) Pinkhas

Mendelevich

born 1884.   article 58-1-10 term 10 end of term 1959.

Nationality Jew   Native of

    Berdichev

Died in the Central Hospital in Block No. 1.   On June

4, 1950 at the hour of 6:10 p.m.

The body was transferred from camp subdivision No 1 to the

place of burial dressed in underclothing laid in wooden coffin on the left

leg of the deceased was tied a tag with the inscription "last name, first

name, patronymic," on the grave was placed a stake with the inscription

Letter No. B-4.

Participants   (Guard Service   Alimova.

in the the burial   {Special section

representatives   (of the Central Hospital Svalovia

  June 7,   1950

ЗИ

СЕКРЕТНО

МВД СССР
Управление
Минлага
СПЕЦОТДЕЛ

19/VI 1950 г.
№ 6/02871

Вх.№ Бюро ЗАГС милиции города Москва бюр-на
Московской области

Форт.

Сообщаем, что заключенный Казакович
(Бер Нистер) Пинхос Менделевич
рожд 1884 года, национальность еврей , умер "4" июня 1950 г.

Причина смерти В поселке Инта Кожвинского района Коми АССР
Последнее место жительства Город города город Москва Московской обл.

Начальник спецотдела управления
Минлага МВД майор   (Каминский)

Начальник 1 отделения   (Мельников)

021594.

Исп. О. Кучеров

SECRET

USSR Ministry of Internal Affairs
Administration
of Mineralnyi Camp
SPECIAL DEPARTMENT

June 12, _____ 195 0

No. _6/02871_

Supervisor of the Department

Head of the Bureau of Civil Status
of the Police of the District _of the City of Moscow_

Moscow Region

City of _____

We report that the convict _Kaganovich_

(Ber Nister) Pinkhos Mendelevich

born in the year _1884_, nationality _Jew_, died on _June 4_ 195 0

In the village of Inta, Kozhvinskii District, Komi Autonomous Soviet Socialist Republic

Cause of death _Heart defect_

Last place of residence _City of Moscow, Moscow Region_

Head of the Special Department of the Administration
of the Mineralnyi Camp of the MVD, Major

021594   (Kaminskii)

Head of Department 1

By _V. Kuganov_   (Mel'nikov)

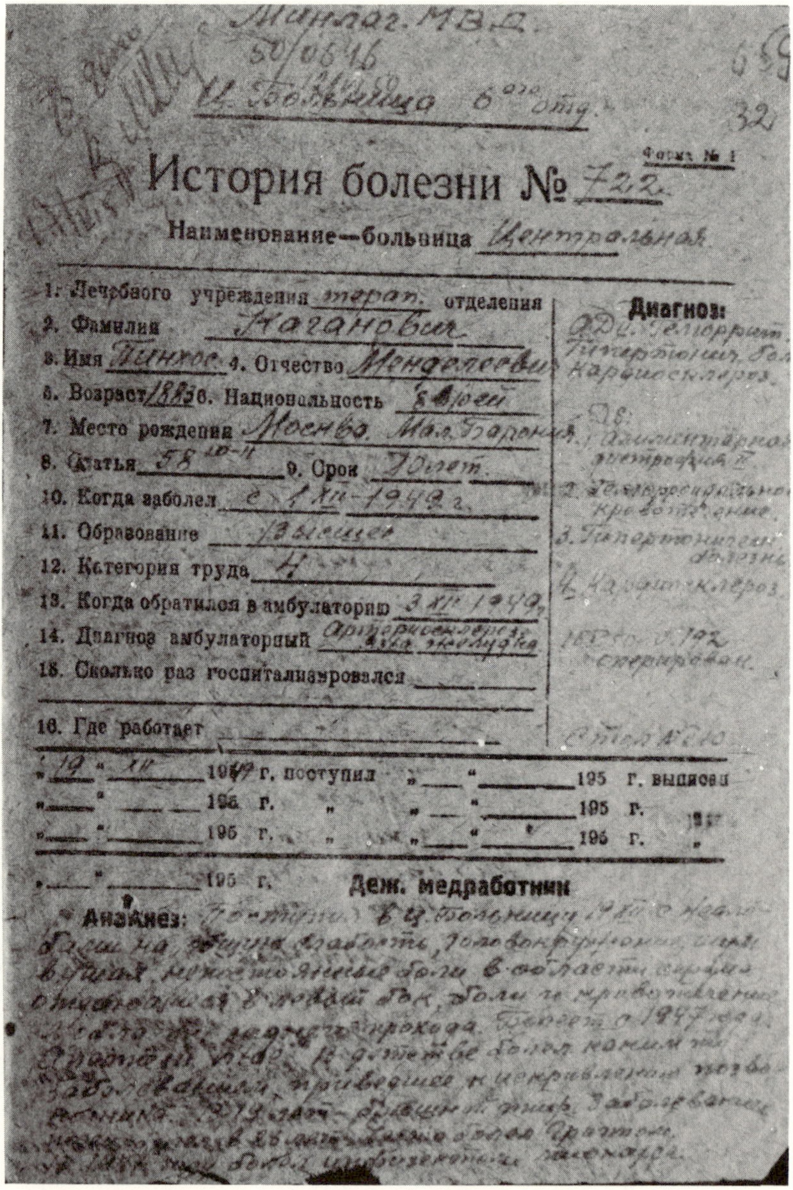

Манлаг. МВД.
50/0646
Ц. больница 6 его отд.

659

32

История болезни № 722

Форма № 1

Наименование—больница _Центральная_

1. Лечебаго учреждения _терап._ отделения
2. Фамилия _Каганович_
3. Имя _Пинкос_ 4. Отчество _Менделеевич_
5. Возраст _1862_ 6. Национальность _Еврей_
7. Место рождения _Москва. Мал. Бронная_
8. Статья _58 10-11_ 9. Срок _10 лет_
10. Когда заболел _с 1 XII 1949 г._
11. Образование _Высшее_
12. Категория труда _И_
13. Когда обратился в амбулаторию _3 XII 1949 г._
14. Диагноз амбулаторный _артериосклероз. язва желудка_
15. Сколько раз госпитализировался _____

16. Где работает _____

Диагноз:
ОД: Гонорит
Гипертонич. бол
Кардиосклероз.

Ж:
1. алиментарная дистрофия II
2. Геморроидальное кровотечение
3. Гипертоническая болезнь
4. Кардиосклероз.

Операрован.

Столяр

_19_ _XII_ 194_9_ г. поступил				195 г. выписан
195 г.				195 г.
195 г.				195 г. 195
195 г.	**Деж. медработник**				

Анамнез: _Поступил в Ц. больницу ..._

[remainder of handwritten anamnez text illegible]

Mineral'nyi Camp of the MVD   6598
50/0646
June 12, 1950
Central Hospital of the 6th Division
Name of Hospital __Central__   Form No. 1
History of illness No. _722_

1. _Therapeutic_ division of the medication institution	**Diagnosis:**
2. Last name _____Kaganovich_____	
3. First name _Pinkhas_ 4. Patronymic _Mendeleevich_	
5. Age _1883_ 6. Nationality ____Jew____	
7. Place of birth _Malaia-Baroniia_ [sic] _Moscow_	
8. Article _58 10-11_ 9. Term _10 years_	
10. When became ill ___from December 1, 1949___	[much illegible writing]
11. Education _Higher_	
12. Category of work ____4____	
13. When came to outpatient deparment _December 3, 1949_	
14. Diagnosis by outpatient dep't _Arteriosclerosis, stomach ulcer_	
15. How many times hospitalized _____	
16. Works where _____	

December 19 _____ 195⁴⁹ **entered** _____ 195

discharged
_____ 195 entered _____ 195 discharged
_____ 195 entered _____ 195 discharged
_____ 195 **Duty medical worker**

Anamnesis:

[much illegible writing]

FRONT

Корпус 8   Камера № 13485

Начальнику Лефортовской тюрьмы МГБ

Прошу вызвать для допроса заключенного

Каганович Пинкос Менделевич

числящегося за *ч по озэ мгб*

Кем вызывается *сл. следовариь*
Ч по озэ моб
Цветаев

Подпись *Цветаев*

ВЫДАТЬ ДЛЯ ДОПРОСА

Деж. пом. нач. Лефортовской
тюрьмы МГБ СССР

„ 9 „ VIII .   1949 г.

BACK

Начало допроса   23 час   50 мин.
Конец допроса   1 час   30 мин.

Приводил на зэ рат. *Хохлов*

Отводил надзир. *Скаряев*

Дежурный по следственному
корпусу надзиратель *Христиф*

FRONT

~~Cell~~ *Office* No. ___8___   Cell No. __134__

To the Head of Lefortovo Prison of the Ministry of State Security

I request that you summon for interrogation the prisoner
_____*Kaganovich Pinkhos Mendelevich*_____
registered under ____*Special Section for Especially Important*____
____*Cases of the Ministry of State Security*____
By whom summoned ____*Senior Investigtor Tsvetaev*____
____*of the Special Section for Especially Important Cases of the*____
____*Ministry of State Security*____

Signature ____*Tsvetaev*____

RELEASE FOR QUESTIONING

Duty Assistant of the Head of Lefortovo
Prison of the USSR MGB   [signature illegible]

_____*August 8*_____ 19 49

BACK

Start of interrogation ___23___ hours ___00___ minutes
End of interrogation _____1____ hours ___50___ minutes

Brought by guard _____*Khokhlov*_____
Taken by guard ___[illegible signature]___

Duty guard for the
        investigative building __[illegible signature]__

INDEX

Agencies for state security, 7

Arrestee Form, 17, K–4/5

Arrest warrants/arrest coupons, 10–11, K–2, K–4/5, M–4

Constitution of 1936, 11, 15

Cover and cover page of personal file, 9–10, M–0, M–1, K–0, K–1

Criminal Procedure Code (1923), 11

"agency of inquiry" provision of, 13–14

extensions of detention under, 25–26, K–12, K–13, K–16, K–19

"measures of restraint" provision of, 14–15, K–3

propaganda/agitation provisions of, 29–30

Death certificates, 38, M–14, K–29, K–30, K–31

Escapes, prisoner, 41

Extensions of detention, 25–26, K–12, K–13, K–16, K–19

Fingerprints, 17–18, M–8, K–6

postmortem, 38–39, M–10

Form No. 1 (camp records), 34–35, M–16

GUGB (*Glavnoe upravlenie gosudarstvennoi bezopasnosti,* Main Administration for State Security), 7, 11, 13

GULAG (*Glavnoe upravlenie lagerei,* Main Administration of Labor Camps), 7, 32

Ianshin, Lieutenant, 37

Interrogation records, 21–25

Ionov, Lieutenant, 32

Kahanovitch, Pinchas Mendelevich ("Der Nister"), 6

Arrestee Form, 17, K–4/5

arrest warrant, 11–12, 16, K–2

burial certificate, 40–41, K–30

Kahanovitch, Pinchas Mendelevich
("Der Nister") *(continued)*
camp record data card, 34–35,
K–27/28
cover and cover page, 9–10, K–0,
K–1
death certificate, 38, K–29
extensions of detention, 25, 26,
K–12, K–13, K–16, K–19
intake fingerprint form, 18, K–6
interrogation records, 21–25,
K–85
labor camp, order to transfer to,
32–33, K–22, K–26
measure of restraint, order on
selection of, 12–15, K–3
medical condition/treatment,
37–38, K–7, K–10, K–14,
K–15, K–17, K–32
Notice affixed to arrest warrant,
31, K–1
official record, K–9
permission to receive items,
20–21, K–18
photograph form, 20, K–25
property, certification on, 35–36,
K–24
search on prison transfer, 19–20,
K–11
search record, 15–16, K–8
Special Board, decision of,
29–30, K–21
Special Board, transfer to being
held for, 31, K–20
special camp, decision to send to,
26–27, K–23
Special Department certificate,
K–31

Kahanovitch, Pinchas Mendelevich
("Der Nister") *(continued)*
transfer record, K–9
Lefortovo Prison, 19, 22, 32
Leonov, Major General, 37

Magadan, 44
Main Administration for State
Security. *See* GUGB
Main Administration of Labor
Camps. *See* GULAG
Mandelstam, Nadezhda, 10, 36,
42–45, M–12
Mandelstam, Osip Emilevich, 5
arrest warrant, 10–11, M–4
camp records (Form No. 1),
33–34, M–16
communications with
correspondence of relatives
about prisoner's death,
43–44, M–13, M–15
correspondence with relatives,
42–45, M–12
cover and cover page, 9, M–0,
M–1
death certificate, 38, M–11
excerpt from record, M–3
Form No. 1 (camp records), M–2,
M–16
intake fingerprint form, 18,
M–8
medical treatment, 36–37, M–9
memorandum, 43, M–14
photograph form, 20, M–6
postmortem fingerprinting,
39–40, M–10

Mandelstam, Osip Emilevich
  (continued)
  prisoner's acknowledgment of
    receipt of decision of Special
    Board, 30–31, M–3
  record of identity, 39–40, M–7
  Special Board, decision of,
    28–29, M–3
  statistical-record card, M–2
  transfer record, 18, M–5
Medical treatment, 36, M–9, K–7,
  K–10, K–14, K–15, K–17
MGB (*Ministerstvo
  gosudarstvennoi bezopasnosti,*
  Ministry of State Security), 7,
  27, 28, 35–36
Money transfers, 42
MVD (*Ministerstvo vnutrennikh
  del,* Ministry of Internal
  Affairs), 7

NKGB (*Narodnyi komissariat
  gosudarstvennoi bezopasnosti,*
  People's Commissariat of
  State Security), 7
NKVD (*Narodnyi komissariat
  vnutrennikh del,* People's
  Commissariat of Internal
  Affairs), 7, 11

Order on selection of measure of
  restraint, 12–15, K–3
Osoboe Soveshchanie. See Special
  Board

People's Comissariat of Internal
  Affairs. *See* NKVD
Photograph forms, 20

Searches, 16, K–11
Solzhenitsyn, Aleksandr, 22, 41
Special Board *(Osoboe
  Soveshchanie),* 27–28
  prisoner's acknowledgment of
    receipt of decision of, 30–31,
    M–3
Special camps, 26, K–22, K–23
Stalin, 10

Transfer records, 18–19, M–5, K–9
Tsvetaev, E., 22
Tsvetaev, Lieutenant Colonel, 27

Zhdanov, Andrei, 10
Zhdanovshchina, 10

❖ ────────────────────────────────

ABOUT THE AUTHOR

Peter B. Maggs is Corman Professor of Law at the University of Illinois College of Law. After graduation from Harvard College and Harvard Law school he studied at the Law Faculty of what is now St. Petersburg State University. He has taught as a Fulbright lecturer at Moscow State University and has worked in the administration of U.S. programs of aid to the legal systems of the newly independent states of the former Soviet Union. He has published numerous books and dozens of articles on Soviet and Russian law.